HOPE
in the Midst of

A HOSTILE
WORLD

George M. Schwab

THE GOSPEL ACCORDING TO
THE OLD TESTAMENT

A series of studies on the lives
of Old Testament characters, written for
laypeople and pastors, and designed to
encourage Christ-centered reading, teaching,
and preaching of the Old Testament

TREMPER LONGMAN III
J. ALAN GROVES

Series Editors

HOPE
in the Midst of
A HOSTILE WORLD

THE GOSPEL ACCORDING TO
DANIEL

GEORGE M. SCHWAB

Apr 2009

PUBLISHING
P.O. BOX 817 • PHILLIPSBURG • NEW JERSEY 08865-0817

Page design by Tobias Design

Typesetting by Lakeside Design Plus

Printed in the United States of America

Library of Congress Cataloging-in-Publication Data

Schwab, George M., 1961–
    Hope in the midst of a hostile world : the Gospel according to Daniel / George M. Schwab.
        p. cm.—(The Gospel according to the Old Testament)
    Includes bibliographical references (p.) and index.
    ISBN-10: 1-59638-006-3 (paper)
    ISBN-13: 978-1-59638-006-6 (paper)
    1. Bible. O.T. Daniel—Criticism, interpretation, etc. 2. Bible. N.T.—Relation to Daniel. 3. Bible. O.T.—Relation to the New Testament. I. Title. II. Series.

BS1555.52.S39 2006
224.5'06—dc22

                                                                2005053548

This book is dedicated to
the men and women
exiled from their homeland and
at war with horns great and small in Babylon,
especially the Dean of Erskine Theological
Seminary, Chaplain (LTC) R. J. Gore Jr.

Come home safely.

CONTENTS

FOREWORD

The New Testament is in the Old concealed;
the Old Testament is in the New revealed.
—Augustine

Concerning this salvation, the prophets, who spoke of the grace that was to come to you, searched intently and with the greatest care, trying to find out the time and circumstances to which the Spirit of Christ in them was pointing when he predicted the sufferings of Christ and the glories that would follow. It was revealed to them that they were not serving themselves but you, when they spoke of the things that have now been told you by those who have preached the gospel to you by the Holy Spirit sent from heaven. Even angels long to look into these things. (1 Peter 1:10–12)

"In addition, some of our women amazed us. They went to the tomb early this morning but didn't find his body. They came and told us that they had seen a vision of angels, who said he was alive. Then some of our companions went to the tomb and found it just as the women had said, but him they did not see." He said to them, "How foolish you are, and how slow of heart to believe all that the prophets have spoken! Did not the Christ have to suffer these things and then enter his glory?" And beginning with Moses and all the Prophets, he explained to them what was said in all the Scriptures concerning himself. (Luke 24:22–27)

The prophets searched. Angels longed to see. And the disciples didn't understand. But Moses, the prophets, and all the Old Testament Scriptures had spoken about it—that Jesus would come, suffer, and then be glorified. God began to tell a story in the Old Testament, the ending of which the audience eagerly anticipated. But the Old Testament audience was left hanging. The plot was laid out but the climax was delayed. The unfinished story begged an ending. In Christ, God has provided the climax to the Old Testament story. Jesus did not arrive unannounced; his coming was declared *in advance* in the Old Testament, not just in explicit prophecies of the Messiah but by means of the stories of all of the events, characters, and circumstances in the Old Testament. God was telling a larger, overarching, unified story. From the account of creation in Genesis to the final stories of the return from exile, God progressively unfolded his plan of salvation. And the Old Testament account of that plan always pointed in some way to Christ.

AIMS OF THIS SERIES

The Gospel According to the Old Testament Series is committed to the proposition that the Bible, both Old and New Testaments, is a unified revelation of God, and that its thematic unity is found in Christ. The individual books of the Old Testament exhibit diverse genres, styles, and individual theologies, but tying them all together is the constant foreshadowing of, and pointing forward to, Christ. Believing in the fundamentally Christocentric nature of the Old Testament, as well as the New Testament, we offer this series of studies in the Old Testament with the following aims:

■ to lay out the pervasiveness of the revelation of Christ in the Old Testament

- to promote a Christ-centered reading of the Old Testament
- to encourage Christ-centered preaching and teaching from the Old Testament

To these ends, the volumes in this series are written for pastors and laypeople, not scholars.

While such a series could take a number of different shapes, we have decided, in most cases, to focus individual volumes on Old Testament figures—people—rather than books or themes. Some books, of course, will receive major attention in connection with their authors or main characters (e.g., Daniel or Isaiah). Also, certain themes will be emphasized in connection with particular figures.

It is our hope and prayer that this series will revive interest in and study of the Old Testament as readers recognize that the Old Testament points forward to Jesus Christ.

TREMPER LONGMAN III
J. ALAN GROVES

PREFACE

My Daniel course met on September 12, 2001, a day after terrorists brought down the World Trade Center, killing about three thousand people. Like everyone else in the country, the students were in shock, trying to make sense of the unthinkable. One said in near hysteria, "We've already lost, since they're willing to die for their beliefs!" Another minimized the horror: "It doesn't matter, since no one cries for the millions who died in slavery." Some saw red: "They're rabid animals fit only to be nuked!" A few agonized, "Shouldn't Christians forgive our enemies?" One student asked, "How can people do such things and think they are acting for God?" On his face was confusion, and he looked to me at the front of the class for an answer.

I began to talk about the book of Daniel. We remember seeing the towers collapse—think of how the Jews felt watching their temple burn and fall to the ground. Their people were killed too, all in the name of Marduk the god of Babylon. The way we Americans felt on that black day echoes the dark and terrible backdrop of the book of Daniel. Daniel himself was a man confused by his sickening visions, living among a people whose wisdom failed them and who could not discern the signs of the times. It is not a lighthearted book useful for cheerfully padding one's eschatological schema. It is a book for confused sufferers who need perspective and solid theological grounding. This characterized the Jews in exile while God's temple lay in ruins. And this characterizes modern-day readers, who read

Daniel for hope and comfort when the world seems to crumble and fall around them.

Jesus is the King of kings, the Son of Man who receives the kingdom. He is the one figure who stands in the place of the saints and whose fate is bound up with theirs. History will be full of rises and falls, terrible wars and rumors of wars, terrorists who target civilians. The people of God groan in this evil world, awaiting their final vindication. It is through this vision of confident hope, in the crucible of the real world, that Christians find Jesus. Not only there, but in the unfolding tragic history of the world, Jesus remains the King over all.

PART ONE

READING DANIEL AS ONE BOOK

Chapter 1 delineates how to approach the narrative and apocalyptic portions of Daniel, and how to outline it (taking into consideration that it is written in two languages). Dating Daniel and the implications for interpretation are at issue in chapters 1 and 2.

The book of Daniel is shown to be a wisdom book in chapter 3, similar in character to Proverbs or Job. One of Daniel's main lessons is that in adversity saints have opportunity to make practical application of their God-inspired wisdom, deeper than the world's wisdom, effective to solve real problems.

Finally, Daniel 1 sets the pattern for the rest of the book. There is a sense in which all of the great issues are seen first in Daniel's opening section. This is discussed in chapter 4.

I

HOW TO READ DANIEL

The book of Daniel comprises two halves—the first, one of the easiest portions of Scripture to understand; the second, one of the hardest. The first is a series of six stories that are obviously meant to convey to the reader, "Go and do likewise." Children around the world are told about Daniel in the lions' den, and are exhorted to "dare to be a Daniel." This use of the stories is appropriate and intended by the author. However, even here there are apocalyptic elements. Nebuchadnezzar's dreams in chapters 2 and 4 are highly symbolic and call for interpretation—in exactly the same way as the second half of Daniel. In the second half, the esoteric dreams and visions also call the reader to identify with the saints and brace for the trials to come. In fact, the stories of the first half could be reckoned as case histories or examples from the experiences of the Jews in exile that flesh out with a concrete sense of reality the second half of Daniel, which speaks with much more generality and abstraction. Yet the stories do not set themselves as programmatic for the future—this is what the apocalyptic section is for. Thus the two halves of Daniel play off one another; both are needed for the book to succeed.

DANIEL AS A COMPOSITE WHOLE

The division of Daniel into two halves is not a simple matter. As noted above, even the stories have apocalyptic elements. A natural division occurs *not* between the stories and the dreams, but one chapter later. Also, there is a major division between chapters 1 and 2. The division is one of language. Chapters 2–7 are written in Aramaic, and chapters 1 and 8–12 in Hebrew. Thus, chapters 2–7 form an Aramaic corpus within the book of Daniel, framed with Hebrew text. One can read the Hebrew chapter 1 as an introduction to Daniel, followed by the Aramaic section, followed by the Hebrew section.

The Aramaic section is a chiasmus, where the first chapter parallels the last, the second relates to the second-to-last, and the middle chapters to each other. (A. Lenglet's outline is shown in figure 1.[1]) Daniel's dream of four beasts (chap. 7), which belongs with the second half of apocalyptic visions, relates to Nebuchadnezzar's dream statue of chapter 2. This links the two halves so that they are not isolated. (Unfortunately, some critics read Daniel as divided in exactly the way it is structured to prevent.)

Figure 1
The Chiastic Structure of Daniel 2–7

A Dream statue representing four kingdoms (chap. 2)
  B Worship the golden statue or perish in a pit (chap. 3)
    C Judgment on Nebuchadnezzar (chap. 4)
    C Judgment on Belshazzar (chap. 5)
  B Worship Darius or perish in a pit (chap. 6)
A Dream of four beasts representing four kingdoms (chap. 7)

In Scripture, only the book of Daniel includes original material written in Aramaic and not Hebrew.[2] Aramaic was the language of Babylon, and continued to be the language of empire until the ancient world was Hellenized under Alexander. The New Testament was written in the new universal language of Greek, as chapters 2–7 of Daniel were written in Aramaic. This was the language of the court of Nebuchadnezzar, and one may imagine court officials such as Daniel recording exceptional annals in that language. In later centuries, all of the Old Testament books were translated into Aramaic (Targums), but these were not confused with the Hebrew originals. The use of Aramaic speaks to the authenticity of the book of Daniel as an exilic document.

DANIEL AS A LITERARY TRADITION— THE GREEK ADDITIONS

I mentioned the writing of this book to an Orthodox priest and his wife, and she responded immediately by asking, "Are you going to treat the Greek portion of Daniel as well?" I responded by saying that most Protestants are unaware that there is a Greek portion. If one were to include the Greek additions to Daniel, then the Daniel corpus would be made up of three languages, not two!

In the centuries following the exile, the Jews produced many writings, often in Greek. Some of these became so closely associated with the book of Daniel that when Daniel was translated into Greek, these stories were included. This Greek translation of the Old Testament was the Bible of the early church—a Bible that included the Greek additions to Daniel. Although not even the Roman church declared these as deuterocanonical until after the Protestant Reformation, and early lists of canonical books such as that of Athanasius do not include them, today they are considered by many outside Protestantism as divinely inspired.

Every Protestant should become familiar with the Greek additions to Daniel for several reasons. First, doing so will help the reader to enter more fully into the mindset of those early Christians who incorporated these additions into their Bible. Second, the additions are regarded as Scripture by much of the Christian world, and as such deserve, at the very least, a reading. Third, they indicate how the book of Daniel was read and regarded in the centuries before Christ. And fourth, 1–2 Maccabees chronicle the events and persecutions of Daniel 11, and flesh out with detail the career of the "little horn," the "king of the North."

There are three additions to Daniel: Bel and the Dragon, Susanna, and the Prayer of Azariah and the Song of the Three Young Men. Bel and the Dragon and the book of Susanna portray Daniel as an ancient Sherlock Holmes, investigating a false accusation by criminal Jewish elders against the godly Susanna, and sleuthing the phony attempt by unscrupulous pagan priests to make the god Bel appear alive. Daniel also debunked the Babylonians' foolish worship of a dragon. These stories show how Daniel was regarded in the centuries preceding the coming of Christ—as a wise man. His chief characterization was as a sage, not a prophet. He explained mysteries, he solved puzzles. This agrees with how we will treat the book of Daniel—as an example of sapiential writing meant to convey and promote wisdom.

The Prayer of Azariah and the Song of the Three Young Men depicts what transpired in the flames of the fiery furnace. Again, this shows how the book of Daniel was regarded in the centuries following the exile. Daniel and his friends were examples to follow, models to emulate. Go and do likewise.

THE DATING AND MESSAGE OF DANIEL

Traditionally, Daniel is regarded as being an exilic, or sixth-century, document. A fifth-century date is within the pale of tradition, allowing for a somewhat later editing process. The alternative view is that it was composed in the Hellenistic era, about four hundred years later.

Some arguments for a late date are as follows. The apocalyptic portion tracks with known history up until the description of the death of Antiochus IV Epiphanes (164 B.C.), where the history goes awry; therefore, that part of the book can be dated to the point in time where the accurate history ends and a real (wrong) prediction begins. So, some or all of the apocalyptic portion was composed very late, about 168–165 B.C. This probably includes the dreams of chapters 2 and 7 as well. Darius the Mede of chapter 6 is unknown to history. He is therefore a figure written into the story by someone who did not know the real history of Persia—obviously much later than a sixth-century date. Nebuchadnezzar's insanity of chapter 4 has no historical basis, but his successor, Nabonidus, was clearly insane. Again, someone must have confused these two kings. Ezekiel refers to a "Daniel"—spelled unlike the biblical Daniel, but like an ancient figure from Ugaritic literature, thus evincing knowledge of an ancient "Daniel" figure known to the Jews (Ezek. 14:12–20; 28:1–3). Perhaps there was no Daniel in the exile, but a later writer invented him using the name from an ancient fable. Further, there are Greek words in the first stories in Daniel—a sure tip-off of a late date, perhaps third century. And in the Hebrew Bible, Daniel is not grouped with the Prophets, but with the later Writings. Perhaps the Aramaic sections are third-century stories that were later supplemented by the Hebrew sections in the mid-second century, and the Daniel corpus continued to grow with the Greek additions.

Of course, the sixth-century date is relatively easy to defend against these criticisms. Daniel was translated into Greek in the mid-second century, 168–163 B.C. How could such a late production, known to be wrong in its predictions, be so quickly accepted as holy writ? It was very popular with the Essenes, and 1 Maccabees quotes it—it was recognized as canonical too early for a mid-second-century date. A good case can be made that the fourth kingdom of chapters 2 and 7 is Rome, which could not have been anticipated in 165 B.C., so even with the late date Daniel still is predicting the future; Antiochus Epiphanes is not the end of the story. In addition, the Greek loan words are mostly in lists of musical instruments—not sufficient to place Daniel in the Hellenistic era; the marvel is that there are so *few* Greek loan words. The book also exhibits an open and friendly attitude toward foreign nations and rulers, unlike genuine second-century materials. As for the argument that the writer did not know his history—Belshazzar was thought a fictional character until the discovery of the Nabonidus Cylinder proved Daniel correct. Daniel deserves the benefit of the doubt, having evinced knowledge of the Persian era beyond any other writer, ancient or modern. A number of suggestions have been offered as to the identity of Darius, not the least of which is that he is none other than Cyrus himself. These observations add up to a unified book early enough to know about Belshazzar and to have been included with other writings as canonical, containing materials that envision a succession of kingdoms far beyond the date of its composition and redaction.

The dating of Daniel impacts its message. If it is essentially a sixth-century document, it demonstrates God's knowledge of the future and power to control the course of history. As events unfold, Jews suffering under malicious kings and kingdoms can take heart that all is on course and according to schedule. This hope did sustain them when times were exceedingly difficult, as is recorded, for example, in 1 Maccabees. No doubt this track record in the community of faith earned the book a place in the Hebrew Bible—and inspired other stories that featured Daniel to be written in Greek. After the coming of Christ, and throughout the church age, Christians have enjoyed that same confidence in their God. They persevere through persecutions and setbacks, secure in the knowledge that God, who foretold events leading up to the first advent of

Christ, can be trusted with events leading up to the second advent—which are also under his sovereign control.

This confident hope is lost if one adopts the late-date model. Events are written down after the fact—no demonstration of God's foreknowledge there. Where true prediction is attempted, the writer gets it wrong. Again, where is the value in that? The stories are not given the benefit of the doubt and are condemned as full of historical inaccuracies; the book cannot speak of the past any more than the future. Its stories are legends or fables purporting to be something that they are not—and the ancient Jews were so credulous that they seemingly placed them in their Bible alongside real prophecy and writings as the word of God.

The present author assumes the early date of writing and seeks to highlight the substantial foundation for faith and trust in the God of Daniel, leading up to the person and work of Christ, and continuing on until all is fulfilled.

FOR FURTHER REFLECTION

1. If you have access to a version of the Bible that includes the Apocrypha, read the book of Susanna. How is Daniel presented there? Consider, in light of this, how you may read Daniel differently.
2. Read Bel and the Dragon, also in the Apocrypha. How might this challenge your expectations of what Daniel is about?
3. God knows your past, as well as your future. How does this fact change the way you deal with adversity?

2

WHY NARRATIVE?
WHY APOCALYPTIC?

Historical plausibility provides Daniel with "punch"—something important would be lost without it. This is especially so in the case of the apocalyptic portion; take away the predictive element and there remains little worth reading. On the other hand, the stories of Daniel were not written to inform the reader about what life was like during the exile.

HOW TO READ THE STORIES

The six stories are highly selective, and the reader is told only enough to make the theological point, which is the real agenda of Daniel. For example, in the accounts of dreams, only elements important to the story are included. Everything else dreamed is not recorded, so any attempt at psychoanalysis on the basis of the dream misses the point. That the historical references in Daniel are defensible does not mean that Daniel should be read as straightforward exilic history. Since the stories are so selective, the reader must concentrate on the theological message being presented.

James Montgomery points out that even though Belshazzar did in fact rule Babylon (thus vindicating Daniel as a historical source), much in the stories still runs contrary to what is known of ancient Babylon and Persia.[1] He observes that a kosher Jew as chief magician would be unworkable; Nebuchadnezzar worshipping Daniel's God over against his own stretches credulity. Instead of events compatible with known history, Daniel presents an adventure book full of excitement and larger-than-life drama. Montgomery suggests the genre "religious romance" to explain this. Although the events happened, Daniel is not about the history of the sixth century; it is about what believers should confess and believe in any century.

If the interpreter's agenda is solely to defend—or to deny—Daniel as a historical source, then the point of the stories might be missed. For example, in chapter 3 the three heroes are in mortal crisis due to their fidelity to God. One might ask, "Where was Daniel?" Various commentaries attempt to answer that by reconstructing possible scenarios. Perhaps Daniel had been called away; perhaps Daniel was not present. Some commentators wisely ignore the question altogether. However, the only worthwhile answer does not reconstruct history, but reads the chapter as literature, as a religious romance. The question becomes, "How does the absence of Daniel change the book?" The other chapters all feature Daniel, his friends sometimes added as sidekicks. By excluding Daniel from chapter 3, it is clear that others besides him were also faithful to God in the face of adversity. The whole book is not therefore about one hero, and a possible misconception of the character of the exile is corrected. *This* is why Daniel is absent from chapter 3. The answer lies with the literary purpose of the story, not with any reconstructed history.

The manner in which theology is implanted into the heart and mind of the believer is through the telling of story. A picture is worth a thousand words. It is one thing to encourage the faithful to stand firm during trials. One may rationally explain that an eternity in heaven is worth suffering now; one may logically delineate the ramifications of the fall and why tribulations are inevitable; one may systematically make all the right arguments. But these lessons pale in comparison to the image of Daniel in the lions' den and the admonition, "Dare to be a Daniel!" In this respect, the stories are very similar to apocalypse.

RE-IMAGING THE WORLD

Apocalyptic literature is produced by oppressed people-groups. Daniel was written by Jews suffering in exile. Revelation was written by and for persecuted Christians. The apocalyptic intertestamental literature was written by Jews under the heel of foreign powers. Even the earlier grandfather of apocalyptic, Mesopotamian apocalyptic literature, was written by an oppressed class.[2] This subjugation helps to explain the hideous images of tyrannical evil and the tortured cries for relief that characterize this material. Salvation is in the distant future. Apocalyptic is designed to comfort the oppressed, to encourage the faithful in distressful times.

Apocalyptic is written for those who feel powerless or helpless, under pressure, marginalized, left out; for those who become the objects of scorn and ridicule for their faith; for those who suffer and cry out, "How long?" It is for anyone who feels burned out and tired, who wonders if life is passing him by. It is for all who grieve, who do not get out of life what they expect, who are frustrated and angry. In a word, apocalyptic is written for those who are in need of *perspective*.

At a recent funeral service, I was asked to read Revelation 21:1–7, about the new heavens and earth, everything made new, and an inheritance for those who endure to the end. Revelation focuses on the conflict between Good and Evil, and who finally wins. One young man occasionally suffered from anxiety and fearfulness late at night; in those times he read Revelation through from beginning to end. The theme that came through loud and clear was *victory*—therefore, there was nothing to fear. This effect on the reader is exactly the opposite of the reaction of those who fear end-time tribulation and so hoard goods and munitions, inspired by their teachers' misunderstanding of apocalyptic.

If John's book were read in one sitting, even though the symbolism would be elusive, the overall message would be clear: God overcomes evil. The one word that cries out from the book is "Hope!" Daniel gives the same message, intertwined with intertestamental history, so that as its meaning unfolds through time, the saints' confidence may increase, not decrease. The book of Daniel was produced in crisis. Reading through it, one cannot miss that, despite appearances, God is in control. The righteous will win in the end.

Suffering and pain are not merely mental experiences, they are also deeply emotional. Larger-than-life images capture this visceral response to extreme circumstances. Apocalyptic helps to ameliorate nerve-wracking anxiety by pointing the victimized community to an otherworldly hope—a salvation not discovered in this place and this time. For this reason, the value or meaning of the symbol is difficult to unpack. Explaining the symbol along rational grounds paints only a pale shadow of the substantial, awe-inspiring Symbol in apocalyptic. In Revelation, the picture of nations drunk on the blood of the martyrs is not something that can simply be exposited! The symbols are intended to have renewing power in the life of the believing community.

Apocalyptic is "addressed to the imagination."[3] It presents a picture of the future, a feel for it, a biased prescience of what it will be like for the saints of God. There is no one-for-one correspondence between the vision and the interpretation. *The visions are interpretations of life.* A Godzilla-like horrific beast would not have the power to seduce—but that is what Rome *is*, despite the grand buildings and awesome army on the march. Reality is not what is visible, but the invisible forces that stand behind history and are seen more clearly in visions than in history books.

For example, recall the terrorist attacks on the World Trade Center towers. In the initial aftermath, Christian and non-Christian alike did not know how to deal with the destruction—and yet they needed to find a meaning in it. Paradigms were thrown at it until it made sense: Osama Bin Laden is the evil that calls for a swift and terrible response; because of homosexuality and abortion, God no longer protects America; Americans should recognize terrorism as a fact of life; opportunities to capture Bin Laden had been squandered; Satan's face could be discerned in the smoke. Each paradigm carried much emotional freight, for a basic human need is to find some kind of sense in suffering. The destruction of the towers and the Pentagon was the mystery; the paradigms tenaciously offered were the desperately needed interpretations. In a similar way, apocalyptic provides a way of making sense of tragic events past, present, and future.

TRANSFORMATION

One way to understand how to read apocalyptic is with the model of a mathematical transformation from the field of communication theory. In the "time domain" a radio signal appears as random fluctuations; various broadcasts are mashed together and cannot be distinguished, as seen in figure 2. In order to discern individual broadcasts, a Fourier transform must be performed. Once transformed

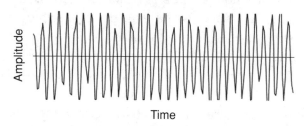

Figure 2
Time Domain of Radio Signal

into the frequency domain, the true character of the radio signal can be readily distinguished, as seen in figure 3. Each radio broadcast can now be tuned to play on a radio. In one domain the signal has one appearance; to see it clearly it must be transformed into another domain. Yet it is exactly the same signal—seen as it appears in two domains.

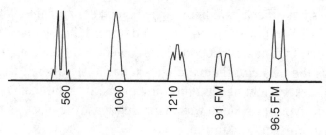

Figure 3
Fourier Transform in Frequency Domain

In Jesus' parable of the sower, there is a literal sower sowing literal seed on four kinds of literal earth. This is the parabolic domain. Once transformed into the existential and historical domain, there is no longer a sower but an evangelist, no longer seed but the word of God, no longer birds but Satan. In John Bunyan's *Pilgrim's Progress*, there is Giant Despair, a "real" monster; when transformed, there is no longer any great threatening creature, but rather despondency and hopelessness. Moses beats Pilgrim with a rod; after transformation there are only guilt and moral failure when trying to keep the law. Crossing a river, when transformed, is Pilgrim's death.

In the domain of the book of Revelation there are lamps, incense, robes, seven heads, 144,000, the mark of the beast, and Satan bound for one thousand years. In the existential and historical domain, there are vital churches (1:20), the prayers of saints (5:8), righteous deeds (19:8), hills and kings (17:10–11), a vast multitude (7:3–9), 666 or man's number (13:18), and the gospel going forth into the whole world and a call to missions (20:1–6). Ezekiel's valley of dry bones or great temple must be transformed into the domain of history and experience—this is its interpretation.

The images must be transformed from the apocalyptic domain into the human existential and historical domain. A picture is worth a thousand words. Apocalyptic takes the teachings of the rest of the Bible and expresses them with unforgettable images. (A sound hermeneutical principle is to interpret unclear passages of Scripture in the light of clear ones, not the other way around.) To suffering saints, sometimes a cold, scientific list of the facts of life does not elicit a movement of the heart toward trust in God; a picture may produce better spiritual fruit. Hope is elsewhere; hope is otherworldly; hope is not rooted in understandable events. God is transcendent; God is close at hand; the future is certain and true.

In the book of Daniel, there is no millennium, no systematic presentation of angelology or demonology, no Satan; and only cryptic and tangential referents to the second advent of Christ and a final oppressor of the saints. Nevertheless, some scholars cannot resist using Revelation as an interpretive grid and importing dispensational theology into the text. For example, Stephen Miller writes in his commentary, "At first glance one might receive the false impression that the resurrection of the righteous and the wicked will occur simultaneously. . . . But this is impossible in light of other Scripture, particularly the parallel passage of Rev 20:4–6."[4] This shows a lack of sensitivity to Daniel. One should ask why the righteous and the wicked rise together in Daniel. What truth does that convey? Miller would vigorously argue that Daniel is "true" when it touches on history, but he flinches when Daniel touches on eschatology! If Daniel is untrustworthy with eschatology, how can it be trusted with history?

Sensitivity to the book of Daniel comes through paying attention to its unique character. For example, there is a reason the name of Yahweh occurs only in the prayer of Daniel and nowhere else in the book. The goal of interpretation should be to feel the force of Daniel, not to flatten it out with assumed theology.

FOR FURTHER REFLECTION

1. How have you tried to find meaning in tragic events?
2. In what ways do the books of Daniel and Revelation help to explain how God can be in control even while bad things happen?
3. How is apocalyptic literature like Jesus' parables?
4. How does apocalyptic imagery touch us on a more visceral level than straightforward doctrinal statements?

3

DANIEL AS A WISDOM BOOK

The book of Daniel can be read as a wisdom book, sapiential literature, alongside of Proverbs, Job, and Ecclesiastes. In the Hebrew Bible, Daniel is not found with the Prophets, but with the Writings, which includes the wisdom books. Some examples of the specialized wisdom vocabulary we find in Proverbs are echoed in Daniel. Words such as *hokmah* ("wisdom"), *bin* ("understanding"), and *sakal* ("wise") occur frequently. Proverbs language is also Daniel language. In Daniel 1:17, God gives the four youths knowledge and *sakal* in all kinds of literature and *hokmah*, and to Daniel he gives *bin* of dreams and visions. In the last chapter (12:3), the end of the world will reveal the brilliance (like the stars of heaven) of the "wise ones" (from *sakal*). Daniel himself is recognized by pagan royalty as one "in whom is the spirit of the holy gods"; he possesses "insight and *sakal* and *hokmah* like the *hokmah* of the gods" (5:11). Ezekiel 28:3 sees Daniel as a wise man first of all, and Daniel is called wise more than anyone in the Old Testament except Solomon.[1]

Ecclesiastes 8:1 reads, "Who is like the wise man? Who knows the *pesher* [interpretation] of things?" The word *pesher*[2] is found in Scripture elsewhere only in the Joseph narrative (14 times) and in Daniel (33 times), in reference to their interpretations of dreams and visions. The ability to interpret mysteries, to solve difficult problems, to discern what God intends to reveal in a matter, is the mark of the wise man. This is the preeminent characteristic of Daniel that Ezekiel appreciates.

REVEALING WHO IS WISE

Interpretation is needed for resolving mysteries. The word for "mystery" or "secret" in Daniel is *raz*. In Daniel 2, the *raz* is the content and meaning of Nebuchadnezzar's dream. It troubled the king because he did not understand it. The Deity was communicating with him, so it was obviously important, but the meaning was elusive. Without knowledge of the purpose of God, the king did not know how to respond, and was fearful of unknown dire consequences. Dreams were part of the mysterious and frightening world of the king, breaking in and terrorizing him.

Nebuchadnezzar's later dream in chapter 4 is also a *raz*, which neither he nor the wise men of Babylon could interpret. Only after God revealed the *pesher* to Daniel did the king understand it. He was relieved to learn the *pesher*, even though it was a terrible warning from heaven. Another mystery to unravel was the markings on the wall made by supernatural fingers in chapter 5. Again, Daniel interpreted these to relieve the king's distress, and the king was happy for this, even though the *pesher* was a death sentence. The fear of the unknown was worse than the message of judgment itself.

Chapters 2, 4, and 5 all set Daniel over against the so-called wise men of Babylon. The question is, who is wise? Where is wisdom to be found? Again and again the legendary wisdom of Babylon is shown to be impotent and worthless, and wisdom from God is revealed as a special gift to those who know him and live faithfully before him. One could argue that the big issue in the book of Daniel is the discernment of the times, the solving of mysteries, and identifying who is truly wise in the world.

The book nears its conclusion in 12:3–4 with a picture of the "wise" who shine like stars in heaven, like angels, forever. This picture contrasts Babylon's wise men, who in futility run helter-skelter to seek elusive knowledge, and their future successors. What distinguishes the saint from the sinner is wisdom and understanding. "Go your way, Daniel, because the words are closed up and sealed until the time of the end. Many will be purified, made spotless and refined, but the wicked will continue to be wicked. None of the wicked will understand, but those who are wise will understand" (12:9–10). The wise are the opposite of the wicked, and true understanding is promised to them. The climax of history as envisioned in Daniel will occur when the truly wise are revealed.

REDEMPTION AND CREATION

Another characteristic of sapiential books such as Proverbs, Job, or Ecclesiastes is the way they downplay themes that are important elsewhere in the Bible. The Bible drinks deeply of redemptive themes and shows how God has worked in history to save his people. But wisdom books approach God differently, pointing to aspects of creation that have not changed over time but that do reveal God's character. For example, God answers Job by pointing to the creation—if God is competent to run the world, then he can be trusted by Job even while suffering. What other answers might God have offered? God could have spoken of his saving deeds, rescuing his people out of Egypt with a mighty hand, his great promises, and so on. Today we would point to Jesus raised from the dead. But in Job, the marvelous creation is an adequate basis for trusting God. In the wisdom books, deliverance from Egypt is not at issue. Neither is covenant with Abraham or Moses or David. The worship at the temple with sacrifices, purity laws, and the prohibition against idolatry is not part of the genius of wisdom books. The law of Moses is not a constitutive element; in fact, "law" in Proverbs is redefined as the wise sayings of the parents (1:8; 3:1; 4:2). Ecclesiastes does not even employ God's covenantal name, Yahweh.

In the book of Daniel, these themes do not find traction either. Daniel is not about God giving or renewing a covenant. It is not about God calling his faithless and recalcitrant people back to himself. It is not about the temple worship, cultic purity, animal sacrifices, or the law of Moses. With the exception of Daniel's prayer of chapter 9, God's covenantal name is not used, nor are the "good guys" even called Israelites, but rather "saints." Daniel approaches God differently than does most of the Bible, having much in common with books such as Proverbs or Job.

Much of what makes the Bible unique in the ancient world is not constitutive of wisdom books. Since distinctive redemptive themes are moved to the back burner, wisdom books look more like the literature of the surrounding nations than does most of the Bible. Sapiential literature has a more international character than other biblical books. Daniel so resonates with non-Israelite culture that half of it is not even written in Hebrew, but in the language of Babylon, Aramaic!

The second half of Daniel is a series of mysterious dreams, a *raz* that needs a *pesher*. Wise men dream and interpret dreams. Wild, symbolic, violent, colorful dreams that are encryptions of reality "behind the scenes" are called "apocalypse," which means "revelation." The second half of Daniel is apocalyptic, and apocalyptic has been associated with wisdom material. Gerhard von Rad lists "eschatological dualism" and "sheer transcendentalism" as characteristics of apocalyptic writings that "purport to be revealed knowledge."[3] In contrast to prophecy, the message of apocalypse does not draw preeminently from God's redeeming acts in history, such as the exodus or the giving of the law.

> Once it is realized . . . that knowledge is the nerve-centre of apocalyptic literature, knowledge based on a universal Jahwehism, surprisingly divorced from the saving history, it should not be difficult to determine the real matrix from which apocalyptic literature originates. This is Wisdom, in which . . . exactly the same characteristics appear.[4]

There is a parallel theological perspective and manner of expression between apocalyptic and wisdom. Both revel in the transcendence of God and speak of the cosmos as revelatory of knowledge. Both emphasize the End of the matter, of one's life, although in different ways. Neither argues from redemptive history. Both use heavy-handed imagery, like the giant goat and ram of Daniel or the leviathan and behemoth in Job. In 1 Enoch dreams and visions of an apocalyptic sort can be regarded as "wisdom encoded in mysterious signs, not the straightforward, empirical wisdom of Proverbs and Sirach."[5]

In other words, what one gains by reading apocalyptic is wisdom. Not wisdom in the form of straightforward nuggets like proverbs, but insight into the way the world works, how God stands behind the creation, how events are guided with moral purpose, and how one equipped with this knowledge should conduct oneself.

Another apocalypse is the Apocalypse of John, the book of Revelation. There, seven times John reminds his readers that the point of the book is to equip the saints to persevere. John introduces himself as one who suffers and patiently endures with all Christians (Rev. 1:9). Jesus says to the church of Thyatira, "I know your . . . perseverance" (Rev. 2:19), and to Philadelphia (Rev. 3:10), "you have kept my command to endure patiently." The terrible vision of the beast from the sea with power to destroy the saints concludes, "This calls for patient endurance and faithfulness on the part of the saints" (Rev. 13:1–10). Dealing with those who worship the beast "calls for patient endurance on the part of the saints who obey God's commandments and remain faithful to Jesus" (Rev. 14:12).

We are given a symbolic glimpse into the workings of the world so that when the hard times come we can endure. In this sense we read the stories and dreams of the book of Daniel as wisdom literature—it is a book designed in such a way that when we are tempted to doubt God's power or goodness, when we see the world crumbling around us, when the World Trade Center towers come down and we are suddenly unsure of the future of civilization, we know God is in control; he will turn it around according to his good purposes. And in the meantime, we should live faithfully before him while history rushes toward its apocalyptic climax.

FOR FURTHER REFLECTION

1. In what ways are Christian answers to today's problems better than the world's?
2. How have setbacks and trouble given you opportunities to exhibit wisdom that comes from God?
3. Have you made the most of these opportunities? Why or why not?
4. How is reading Daniel as a wisdom book agreeable to the additions to Daniel?

4

THE PARADIGM

Daniel 1 sets the pattern for the rest of the book of Daniel. It is Daniel's own introduction, and it is important not to rush through it. This is where the reader is introduced to God, and the only place in the book where God is said to act directly.

WHAT GOD DOES IN HISTORY

Throughout the rest of Daniel, the omniscient narrator goes out of his way *not* to ascribe direct action to God. Outside of the first chapter, God is not an actor in the stories; he is transcendent, and his actions are mediated through his agents. Rather than say, "God revealed the *raz*" (2:19), the text says "the *raz* was revealed." Not "God restored my sanity" but "my sanity was restored" (4:36). "Darius the Mede took over the kingdom" rather than "God gave Darius the kingdom" (5:31); "The understanding of the message came to him" rather than "God revealed the understanding of the message" (10:1). Wherever action *is* ascribed to God, it is mediated through a character in the story, not through the omniscient narrator, such as when

Daniel tells Darius about God sending an angel to close the lions' mouths. We learn about it secondhand. This is true throughout the stories and the apocalyptic section of Daniel—God is not a character in the unfolding drama.

But this mode of writing that avoids ascribing direct action to God is *not* true of chapter 1. Here God is said to have directly accomplished three things, and these three things are programmatic for the rest of the book of Daniel and for all of history itself: God handed Jehoiakim over to Nebuchadnezzar the king of Babylon, God gave the Jewish youths favor with the official, and God gave them impressive wisdom. These three things are constitutive elements in the future course of history.

The saints will, throughout time, be subject to hostile powers; they do not normally hold the reins of power. Usually, however, they enjoy a measure of favor until the end of this oppression and the ushering in of God's kingdom. This is glimpsed in the vindication of the Jews in Daniel 3 and 6. During this time, the saints will be given wisdom beyond their peers (1:20). Oppression is an opportunity for the vindication of the wisdom of God.

VINDICATION OF THE SAINTS

In each of the stories to follow, the accused are vindicated in the end. Even after they have passed the point of no return, they are revealed to be guiltless and in favor with God. The powerful sovereigns are shown to be condemnable and must repent and change. And in the apocalyptic section, the confident hope is the saints' vindication when God's kingdom fills the earth; mere earthly kingdoms will, on a cosmic scale, be shown false and failing.

Another word for vindication is "justification." To be vindicated is to be justified, to be found righteous. Consider 1 Timothy 3:16:

Beyond all question, the mystery of godliness is great:

> He appeared in a body,
>> was vindicated by the Spirit,
> was seen by angels,
>> was preached among the nations,
> was believed on in the world,
>> was taken up in glory.

Jesus was vindicated (*dikaioō*)—in other words, justified— by being declared righteous through his resurrection. Justification for sinners is to be declared righteous because Jesus is righteous. Jesus was raised from the dead, proving that he is favored by God and found righteous. His death was a great injustice, the greatest injustice ever perpetrated, and thus Jesus could not stay dead. Justification in this case is being declared righteous before one's enemies in the face of unjust treatment. It is God announcing once and for all who is righteous.

All that is Jesus' is ours, and in his resurrection he is clearly declared righteous before God. Insofar as Christians share in his resurrection we also share in his vindication. Thus the whole theme of vindication in the book of Daniel points forward to Christ and anticipates his resurrection. Without Christ, these are simply stories. With Christ in view, Daniel becomes an illustration of the way Jesus' church shares in his death and resurrection (Rom. 6:5).

REVERSAL

Another theme introduced in Daniel's paradigmatic first chapter is that of *reversal*. The story progresses in one direction until suddenly the reader is surprised by an unexpected turn of events. This is seen in the food incident. The young men are described as being without blemish (*mum*) in

Daniel 1:4. In Canticles 4:7 the girl is "without flaw," speaking of her physical beauty. But the word is also used in Leviticus, Numbers, and Deuteronomy to describe unblemished animals fit for ceremonial use, that is, to sacrifice before the Lord. The use of *mum* might be intended to evoke the temple worship which had been destroyed by Nebuchadnezzar. The young men were ceremonially pure, fit for service before God, and this purity is seen in their resistance to eating the king's rich food (*patbag*). They requested from their "guardian" (*meltsar*, which the King James Version takes as a proper name, "Melzar") to be tested with vegetables and water for ten days. After ten days, they were fatter and healthier than the others, so they were allowed to continue on their diet.

The obvious purpose here is to show an unexpected and miraculous reversal and vindication of the young men. Against all reason and expectation, the young men were healthier. In biblical passages like the Elijah and Elisha narratives, critics sometimes go to absurd lengths to take a miraculous story and provide a naturalistic explanation. For example, Elijah is said to have started the bonfire at the altar of Yahweh in the contest against Baal by secreting napalm into it and igniting it with a mirror! Evangelicals rightly reject this kind of treatment and affirm the miraculous. However, it is curious that evangelical conservatives who write commentaries on Daniel sometimes behave just like these critics and offer naturalistic explanations for miracles and dreams! Perhaps they intend to make Daniel seem more believable. But in the process of trying to affirm its historicity, commentators should be careful not to miss its message. The story says nothing at all about the importance of a good diet or nutrition. The *patbag* was the rich food, the good stuff; the vegetables were not expected to yield good results. The youths were fatter despite eating inferior food. The text speaks to the superiority of remaining faithful to God over against compromise, not to the superiority of vegetables![1] This is of one piece with the later reversals in Daniel, the "surprise!" element when God wins after his enemies seem to have vanquished the saints. Reversal is perhaps the principal message of Daniel that unites all the stories together with the apocalyptic portion. The saints in the end will be vindicated and rewarded; when the evil power reaches its zenith, it will be cut off.[2]

Who is in charge, the great and powerful despots, or the Most High God? The apocalyptic portion takes the stories and shows that they are typical of all history, history which plays out this struggle climaxing in a final conflict. The saints then inherit the kingdom. Take heart, all you saints! In the midst of threats and opposition, there is hope. There is hope!

Of course, the ultimate reversal of all time is seen in the death and resurrection of Jesus Christ. His enemies thought they had won because he died. But the Great Reversal is that he rose from the dead, triumphing over the cosmic powers that motivated his enemies. Along with Jesus, someday all Christians will join him in this Great Reversal. In the meantime, the saints suffer opposition while taking the opportunity to show forth in the world the wisdom of the gospel.

THE WISDOM OF BABYLON

The Hebrew youths were trained in the wisdom of Babylon. This involved being acquainted with polytheistic writings and occult practices, astrology, divination, and magic—knowledge forbidden in Israel. It was spiritual *patbag*, the educational equivalent to Nebuchadnezzar's rich food. The youths became experts in the occult, learned in the lore of Babylon. Their education was intended to alienate them from their Israelite culture. Their Yahwistic names were changed to the names of pagan gods. Azariah ("Yahweh is my help") became Abednebo ("Servant of Nebo"). This is so heinous that the book of Daniel deliberately corrupts the name of the god from "Nebo" to "Nego"; it is intolerable that a faithful Jew wear the name of a false deity. Hananiah ("Yahweh is gracious") became Shadrach ("Command of Aku," a Sumerian moon-god). Mishael ("Who is what God is?") became Meshach ("Who is what Aku is?"). And Daniel ("My Judge is God") became Belteshazzar ("Belitu[3] protect the king"). The only difference between this and the king of chapter 5, Belshazzar, is a single phoneme, "te." Perhaps this is another deliberate corruption of a name designed to distance Daniel from the pagan deity and the pagan king.[4] A tablet has been discovered from ancient Babylon that lists a "Belshazzar" as an official of the king—perhaps this person is our Daniel. With the exception of the (modified) names, no god is ever mentioned by name in Daniel except Yahweh.

The youths were expected to eat new foods, were given new names, and forced to learn the culture of Babylon. They were being systematically indoctrinated and distanced from their Israelite heritage. At the end of this process they would no longer be Jews, but Babylonians. They would have new identities. Daniel 11:26 identifies those who eat a king's *patbag* with his closest advisors. At the end of this process, Nebuchadnezzar himself examined the Hebrew youths and found them to be ten times better than the wise men of Babylon. They were experts in the arts of the Chaldeans. Perhaps this is another reversal analogous to the physical test of food. Just as Jewish food made the youths more fit for service to a pagan king, so also did Jewish faith. The wisdom of the youths is their defining characteristic in Daniel 1:4. They are described as "showing aptitude [*sakal*] for every kind of learning [*hokmah*], well informed [*da'at*], quick to understand [*bin*]." God gave them wisdom, skill, and understanding (Dan. 1:17). And this wisdom was put into service in the court of Nebuchadnezzar.

The relationship between Daniel and Babylonian wisdom is a complex one. On the one hand, the book of Daniel is more or less friendly to foreigners. It shows Nebuchadnezzar commending the Most High God to the whole world in 4:1–3. Daniel seems to have had a heartfelt concern for the king (4:19). Darius (6:14) made every effort to save Daniel, and was so distressed at Daniel's predicament that he could not sleep. This friendly attitude is unlike the later postexilic attitude we see in the intertestamental works like 1–2 Maccabees.

Similarly, the wisdom of Babylon is never directly criticized or mocked; it is simply shown to be impotent and worthless. Only the God-given wisdom of Daniel was able to interpret the dreams of the king; the wise men could not do it. Their wisdom was unable to solve the problems of their day. Daniel did not draw on his education for answers, but in faith, as he looked to the one God, the answers were forthcoming. Although the apostle Paul was well educated, he says that the gospel he preached was folly to the philosophically minded Greeks, and yet it showed forth wisdom from God deeper than any earthly wisdom. Jesus has become our wisdom (1 Cor. 1:20–30). Although Christians today may be highly educated in the best schools, they are truly wise only if they take every thought captive to Christ (2 Cor. 10:5).

DANIEL AS ROLE MODEL

Daniel's integrity and reputation are never impugned by his indoctrination into the Babylonian elite. There is no guilt by association. Far from it. He and his companions are the heroes of this period in Jewish history, heroes intended to be imitated. The reader is invited to imitate the faithful Jews and to identify with them. They had seen it all, everything Babylon had to offer, and had rejected their new identities. They remained true to their heritage even while being of great service and importance in the pagan kingdom. The reader is expected to go and do likewise.

The three companions of Daniel were cast into the fire, and every exiled Jew was in the "furnace" of Babylon, being tested along with those three. As they came out safely, so also we, as a people, will come out. Thus the moral qualities the three exhibited are relevant to every exiled believer.

In chapter 9 Daniel prays a model prayer. This is the only place in Daniel where there is interest in typical redemption themes. Daniel calls on Yahweh and confesses the sins of Israel, standing in the place of every Israelite. Again, the reader is expected to go and do likewise—pray along with Daniel the prayer of faith, hold unswerving in the lions' den, resist the demands by great powers to give up one's identity as a person of faith, be truly wise. Present your body as a living sacrifice, without blemish; do not be conformed to the world, but be transformed by the renewal of your mind to prove what is the will of the Most High God (Rom. 12:1–3).

John Calvin, who was also an exile in a foreign land, wrote this: "There was an angelic holiness to Daniel, yet he was dragged off ignominiously into exile and was brought up among the king's eunuchs. If this happened to such a holy man, who from boyhood had devoted himself entirely to piety, what indulgence is it that God should spare us!"[5]

Daniel is an example for Christians. We can look at our hardships and our sufferings for the name of Christ and identify with Daniel who also suffered. "And what more shall I say? I do not have time to tell about . . . prophets, who through faith . . . shut the mouths of lions, quenched the fury of the flames" (Heb. 11:32–34). Their faith strengthens us in our trials.

Sunday school teachers are quite right when they encourage children to dare to be a Daniel. It is for this reason that the stories were written and have been preserved. They are intended to inspire great faith in the midst of great trials, great hope in the face of great opposition, great confidence when the wisdom of this world would counsel despair.

FOR FURTHER REFLECTION

1. How do Christians compromise today? What is real compromise, and what is avoiding unnecessary hindrances to seekers?
2. Into what kinds of "wisdom" can a person today be educated?
3. What kinds of questions or problems do these pursuits of knowledge seek to answer? Should Christians be engaged in seeking solutions to these problems?
4. What are the seductive aspects of these areas of knowledge? Do Christians necessarily become corrupted by non-Christian ways of thinking when they engage in these activities? How effective have these areas of study been?
5. In what ways do Christians await vindication today?
6. Where did Daniel's fearless confidence come from? Why was the official fearful in contrast?

PART TWO

THE ARAMAIC PORTION:
THE GOLD AND SILVER AGES

After the paradigmatic opening chapter of Daniel, the language of the book switches from Hebrew to Aramaic. The Aramaic portion describes life in the royal court of Nebuchadnezzar, Belshazzar, and Darius. These carefully written and chosen stories paint an unforgettable picture of fidelity in the face of evil, of wisdom displayed before counterfeits, of proud kings brought low. Part Three covers the portion of Daniel that reverts back to Hebrew, and the period of time corresponding to the Bronze Age of Nebuchadnezzar's dream.

God does not leave himself without a witness, and even the great Nebuchadnezzar sees with his own eyes one like a son of God—willing and able to deliver his people. The empty boasts and claims of proud monarchs are vividly portrayed in the annals of Daniel. These serve as an anchor for the later visions and dreams that treat such kings in a much more symbolic and abstract way. Once one has been exposed to Belshazzar and Darius, one may easily believe in a future boastful "little horn" wearing out the saints.

5

NEBUCHADNEZZAR'S HEAD

Daniel 2 treats Nebuchadnezzar's terrible nightmares. Immediately in the story, the ineffectiveness of the wise men is demonstrated, and Nebuchadnezzar himself declares them to be frauds. After Daniel seeks God in prayer, the interpretation (*pesher*) of the mystery (*raz*) is revealed to him. Daniel explains the *pesher* to the king after making it clear that the solution has nothing to do with the discredited Babylonian magicians. Nebuchadnezzar glorifies God in response.

MANTIC DREAMS

Here again modern commentators are prone to give psychotherapeutic explanations to the dreams, as if this helps affirm the text's authenticity. Nebuchadnezzar is said to be anxious about the fragility of his kingdom, worried about his political staying power. Thus the dreams were revelatory of his subconscious and emotional state. However, when Daniel offered his counsel, he did not say (with these commentators), "There is a God in heaven who revealed to me that your dreams are a symptom of your psychological distress due to anxiety."

Mantic dreams are, by contrast, revelatory of the future; Daniel's own dreams accurately predicted events centuries later. In Genesis 41, Pharaoh had dreamed of seven fat and seven lean cows—this was not symbolic of his own fears, but of fourteen years of agricultural fortune. The meaning of Joseph's dreams was immediately recognized by his family (Gen. 37:5–11). Nebuchadnezzar's dreams belong in the same class as the handwriting on the wall in Daniel 5. Belshazzar's anxiety over the surrounding Median army certainly did not produce the dreaded inscription (although even this is given a naturalistic explanation by Joyce Baldwin).[1]

In antiquity, most dreams were recognized as a reflection of one's state of mind. But "message dreams," which were a divine revelation, were in a different class from the ordinary. Dreams of this kind were revealed to the leader in crisis situations. They were written down only if an interpretation was available from the divine realm. Mantic dreams were recorded in a highly formatted way, preserving only those elements appropriate to the genre. This stylized presentation is not amenable to psychoanalysis, and is not reflective of the emotional state of the dreamer.

First, the setting and circumstances of the dream are recorded. Sometimes the king slept at the feet of the image of his god to try to produce a revelation from the deity. (Solomon did this in 1 Kings 3:4–5, and God met him in a dream, promising wisdom.) Next, the content of the dream is relayed. The dreamer suddenly awakens with an intense memory of the dream. Contact between the divine and human realms is so traumatic to humans that the blow is softened somewhat through the medium of dreams. Even then, the dreamer is terrorized and shaken to his core. Finally, the reaction to the dream and its fulfillment are recorded. Nabonidus records many dreams in Babylonian inscriptions that date to a point in time close to Nebuchadnezzar and that use language similar to Daniel 4:19: Daniel "was greatly perplexed for a time, and his thoughts terrified him. So the king said, 'Belteshazzar, do not let the dream or its meaning alarm you.'"

The message of the dream was expressed symbolically. A dream-interpretation manual that lists various images and their meanings has been unearthed in Susa, the ancient capital of Persia. For example, if the dreamer eats a hyena, he will have an evil seizure; if he eats a beaver, there will be a rebellion; if he sits on any number of things, various results will follow; if he receives various gifts, meanings are specified for each; and so on. Once the dreamer awakens, he immediately communicates the dream's content to anyone nearby. It becomes vitally necessary to decode it, because not knowing its meaning is worse than any pronounced judgment might be.[2]

The dreams that prognosticate the future come from Daniel's God. They demonstrate not only God's absolute control over and knowledge of events, but also that these events will proceed according to a plan. Since God is in control, the saints can hope for the future even if the present is dominated by hostile powers. The course of history will continue, commanded by arrogant nations, until the kingdom of God is established. This kingdom is a Rock, not made with human hands, and therefore not the same kind of kingdom such as earthly kings rule. It will grow and grow until it fills the earth, replacing the powers of this world. Therefore, saints, take heart! But also, the rulers of this world ought to be humble before this God. In Nebuchadnezzar's courts, only God's messenger was able to interpret the times, to give meaning to the confusion. Even though the message was not what was desired, the God-given insight gave the king peace. God's wisdom was displayed.

Christians are able to proclaim this same message around the world: the King is coming; his kingdom will fill the earth. Wise rulers even today will give heed to this insight and not stand in his way. Christians can also take heart from Daniel in that we are part of the fulfillment of the dream as we participate in the growing church, which starts small as the smallest seed yet grows into a great tree to fill and give shade to the earth.

THE *PESHER*

Daniel gave the interpretation to Nebuchadnezzar. Each segment of the dream-statue represented a different future kingdom. The head of gold, said Daniel, is Nebuchadnezzar and his glorious Babylonian kingdom. The upper body of silver is a kingdom to follow, as are the bronze midriff and the iron legs.

Keep in mind that this revelation was tantamount to saying that the United States would fade away as a world power and be replaced by a less glorious kingdom, and this process would continue until a much harder and more terrifying power would emerge, inferior to the United States in resplendence but tougher and more brutal. American culture would be a thing of the past, and the world would not care any longer about today's way of life. What would be the reaction to a pronouncement such as this? At first, Nebuchadnezzar was happy, since the mystery was solved, and thus, manageable. But as time went on (in chapter 3 of Daniel), his attitude changed, and he took futile steps to ensure that his kingdom would last forever. Christians today might ask themselves if they would be happy to see the kingdom of God come in to replace their own indigenous cultures. What aspects of the culture might have to be given up? Would citizens be happy about this? Neither was Nebuchadnezzar.

Daniel described a progression of four kingdoms to be followed by the establishment of God's kingdom. Three ways of reading this will be presented below. Each has its strengths and weaknesses. The head of gold is, as all agree, Nebuchadnezzar's Babylonian Empire. This is followed by two intermediate kingdoms of silver and bronze, culminating in a complex iron empire, divided into two legs, with feet of iron mixed with clay.

The first view, which might be called the unconventional view, seeks to interpret Daniel 2 in the light of the later chapters of Daniel. In chapter 11 we again are treated to two vying kingdoms that share a common material culture. These are ruled by the king of the North and the king of the South, and all agree these are the Seleucid and Ptolemaic kingdoms, both part of what was once Alexander's Greek kingdom. Daniel 11:14–19 speaks of this bifurcated kingdom. Daniel 2:41 interprets the iron legs to be a divided kingdom. What is especially interesting is Daniel 11:17, the reference to the failed marriage alliance. This is reminiscent of Daniel 2:43, which says that the two kingdoms will "mingle themselves with the seed of men" (KJV), or "will mix with one another in marriage" (RSV), but it will not stick, as clay does not mix with iron. Thus Daniel 11 seems to be talking about the same kingdom(s) as the iron legs of Daniel 2, the Ptolemaic and Seleucid dynasties. Both chapters 2 and 11, then, end with the same time period. Two great empires did arise between Nebuchadnezzar and Alexander (the Medes and the Persians), empires that Daniel elsewhere mentions by name. After Belshazzar (of the kingdom of gold) died, Darius *the Mede* inherited the kingdom (chap. 6); after Darius, Cyrus *the Persian* took the kingdom (Dan 6:28). So all four kingdoms are described in Daniel: head of gold = Babylon; torso of silver = Media; midriff of bronze = Persia; and legs of iron = the split kingdom of Alexander. The Rock = the kingdom of God which follows in the Maccabean revolt against Greek culture and the reestablishment of pure temple worship. The kingdom of God was ushered in by driving the pagans out and rededicating the temple.

This unconventional view has not been embraced by most evangelicals.[3] It has a number of weaknesses. First of all, Media and Persia were not separate political kingdoms that sequentially followed one another. The metals of silver and bronze would have to indicate race and culture rather than political differences in this case, which of course was not true of the transition from gold to silver or from bronze to iron. This interpretation, then, makes Daniel look like an incompetent historian. To the contrary, Daniel did in fact know the politics of this period, since elsewhere he treats the Medo-Persian Empire as a unit (Dan. 5:28; 6:8, 28). In addition, Christians understand that the kingdom of God came with Christ, not with Judas Maccabeus, and in Jesus' day the Romans ruled Palestine. Nothing at all came from the Maccabean revolt; after them the Roman Empire dominated the world—and again, Daniel would be entirely mistaken about history if he thought world history would end with Alexander's empire. He did not believe this in fact, since in 11:18 he envisions a power to challenge the Seleucids, which of course can only be Rome.

However, an honest reader cannot lightly set aside the affinity that is drawn in Daniel between the Greek kingdoms of chapter 11 and the iron legs of chapter 2. If they are not talking about the same political entity or period of history, at the very least one must acknowledge that they are similar in character, that they look the same.

The traditional way of reading chapter 2 is to see the silver torso as the singular Medo-Persian Empire, the bronze midriff as the Greek Empire, and the iron legs as the Roman Empire. The Rock is the kingdom of God ushered in by Jesus and the proclamation of his gospel. Figure 4 coordinates the visions of chapters 2, 7, and 8, along with their interpretations. The goat is specifically identified with Greece, and the ram is Medo-Persia (8:20–21). Daniel goes over the same periods of history from different angles, once as metals in a statue, again with one set of beasts, and then with another; once as spiritual warfare between powers in heaven, and again with detailed descriptions of wars between kings. In the same way, the book of Revelation goes over the same events from different perspectives (seven bowls, seven trumpets, seven seals, etc.).

Figure 4
The Traditional View of Daniel's Four Kingdoms

Chapter 2	Chapter 7	Chapter 8	The *Pesher*
Gold head	Winged lion		Babylon
Silver torso	Bear	Ram	Medo-Persia
Bronze midriff	Leopard	He-goat	Greece
Iron legs	Indescribable beast		(Rome)
Supernatural Rock	Heavenly court		God's kingdom

A third way of reading chapter 2 notes that the unconventional and traditional views cancel each other out. Even with hindsight, thousands of years later, there still is no clear consensus among evangelicals on which is right (although most opt for the traditional). Perhaps Daniel does not intend to precisely forecast the future. "The vision intends to communicate something more general, but also more grand: God is sovereign; he is in control despite present conditions."[4]

> People miss the point when they spend time arguing over who the empires were. For the recipients of the book what mattered was that they lived during the fourth regime, and when successive generations have reapplied the scheme of empires to the history of their day, in principle they responded to the vision

in the way it sought. If for them the fourth empire is Britain or America or Israel or some other, then the vision applies to it.[5]

Although Daniel does get specific (see chap. 11) about future events, the interpretation of the dream does not really hang on the proper identification of the kingdoms, and even less on the identity of the ten toes, the two legs, and so on, as long as the Rock is correctly understood. Jesus established his kingdom upon his death and resurrection. Jesus identifies himself (the son of the owner of the vineyard) with this Rock (Luke 20:14–19), and combines this image with that of the rejected stone from Psalm 118:22, creating the metaphor of a rejected stone (Jesus being rejected) as the most important stone, the stone that will crush his enemies (the religious leaders), as the Rock in Daniel crushes the kingdoms of the earth, making them like chaff which the wind drives away (Dan. 2:35). In the final estimation, the kingdoms of the earth, including the iron legs, are all who oppose the gospel and resist the kingdom of God, which grows to fill the earth (2:35).

Daniel told Nebuchadnezzar that he was the golden head. The head was the king—and the kingdom. In a profound way, the king is united with the diverse peoples that made up the kingdom. This is also true of the kingdom of God. Jesus is the kingdom by virtue of being the King. The coordination of king and kingdom is seen elsewhere in Daniel, for example, in 7:13–22 where the "one like a son of man" seems to be an individual but also an embodiment of the saints. One can never separate Christ from the kingdom of God; this kingdom cannot be built on earth without its King and his gospel preached and believed.

We now live in the days predicted by Daniel, the days when the Rock not made with hands is growing into a great mountain and filling the earth. Jesus is the foundation of the church, and the wise build their house on the Rock of his words (Matt. 7:24–27). The fool ignores this Rock and builds his life on sand, predestined by his own folly to great ruination. Christ is the stumbling stone, the Rock that made Israel stumble and fall (Rom. 9:30–33) because they pursued righteousness through their own accomplishments (works) and not through believing in Christ.

In the same way, Nebuchadnezzar tried in chapter 3 of Daniel to answer God's revelation through his own achievement, rather than yielding to God's plan. Today people must be careful not to make the same mistake. Nebuchadnezzar thought that he could establish himself by great achievement; the chief priests and scribes thought that by doing good works they would gain God's favor; the foolish man builds his house on the sand of his own philosophy. Nebuchadnezzar's attitude was insane (Dan. 4:30–33), the chief priests and scribes were rejected by God, and the foolish man will not withstand the storms of life. Therefore, build your house on the Rock! Embrace God's revelation and be a citizen of his kingdom! Believe in the gospel of Jesus and be saved! Else your fall will likewise be great.

THE WISDOM OF BABYLON

In the book of Daniel, the truly wise build their house on the Rock of God's revealed will; the pseudowise build their house on the dubious learning of the Chaldeans. On the one hand, the Babylonian sages did effectively realize what the problem was—a divine communication that needed interpretation. Daniel stood side by side with them in full agreement about the nature of the problem that they all faced. However, the Magi were utterly incompetent to solve it. The pagan professionals could not help, and Daniel did not draw upon their accumulated techniques when he told the king the interpretation. And his interpretation could not have been popular with the courtiers of Babylon.

When Christians today face social problems of various kinds—when people are troubled by the confusion of their world—to whom do they turn for answers? Do they turn to ineffective advisors who can offer nothing more than the wisdom of this world, who in the end encourage the sufferer to build his house on the sand, or to trust in his own achievement, or to try harder to be better? When Christians are tasked with helping such a sufferer, will their counsel be indistinguishable from that of the world? Will you offer only the wisdom of the professional sages of today? Will you counsel sand? Or will you speak the gospel with words inspired by God, lifting bowed head to contemplate God's advancing kingdom?

FOR FURTHER REFLECTION

1. What does it mean to be a citizen of heaven? How does this affect modern Christians' sense of nationalism or patriotism? Who is our King?
2. What is the source of your wisdom? Does the wisdom of this world help?
3. What does prayer accomplish? Does Daniel pray alone? What is the significance of this?
4. What has disturbed and shaken you in much the same way that Nebuchadnezzar's dream disturbed him?
5. What is Daniel's reaction to the revelation from God?

6

NEBUCHADNEZZAR'S FEAT

D aniel 3 is abruptly juxtaposed with chapter 2 because there is a logical connection between them—the reader is meant to see this as Nebuchadnezzar's response to his dream and its interpretation. Even though he had praised God at the end of chapter 2 as a revealer of mysteries, he did not really accept his own mortality, and created an image entirely of gold in rebellion against the vision of Babylon limited to a head of gold in world history. Nebuchadnezzar erected a golden "image," Aramaic *tselem*, the same word as used in his dream of Daniel 2:31, highlighting the equation between them.

Nebuchadnezzar's plan was to cement his kingdom by forcing all peoples on earth to bow down before the *tselem* in unison when the music played. Daniel's three friends, however, refused to participate. Faithful Jews cannot be made to willingly bow before an image. Nebuchadnezzar's officials maliciously accused these Jews of not cooperating. The actual idiom used in Daniel 3:8 is that the officials "ate the pieces of the Jews." This phrase is a dark foreboding of the lions' den in chapter 6. Nebuchadnezzar, in a furious rage, questioned the disobedient Jews, and they affirmed that they would never bow down. The *tselem* of the king's face changed, and he ordered that they be cast bound into the fiery furnace. But when he looked into the flames, he saw the three walking around with a fourth, like a son of God. The king called them out, and praised God for delivering his servants. The three were promoted.

UNIVERSAL IDOLATRY

Idolatry is treated differently in Daniel than in other parts of the Bible. No god is named in Daniel, and the book goes out of its way to avoid ascribing names to them (3:12; 4:8; 5:4; 11:37). The *tselem* of chapter 3 does not stand in the place of Babylonian gods such as Marduk or Bel. The only qualifier is the repeated acknowledgement that Nebuchadnezzar made it (3:1, 2, 3, 5, 7, 14, 18). It is his achievement; to bow before it is to worship the king's masterpiece. It is his magnificent feat. To bow before the Feat of Nebuchadnezzar is to bow before the head of gold in the *tselem* of chapter 2. This is idolatry stripped of religion. It is no longer a divine being at issue in worship; it is the feat of a man.

Idolatry of this sort is shown by Daniel to be dangerous in that it claims exclusive adherence from every citizen. This makes Daniel 3 eerily similar to the secularized society that, sadly, defines our contemporary age. Today, of course, religious symbols or a shared religious perspective is not used to promote societal unity. Indeed, tolerance of great variety is at present a social virtue. But contemporary culture does make judgments on the basis of conformity to other norms, one of which is the very virtue of tolerance! If one were to claim that biblical standards were applicable to all people, one might be marginalized or disqualified for public office. If one were to say, "Jesus is the only way," one might be labeled a fundamentalist bigot, suspiciously narrow-minded, or uncharitable.

Revelation 13:11–18 speaks of the world as ruled by a beast-like government, impressive and monstrous, loyalty to which was tested with an image (13:14). The people were marked with the number 666, which is interpreted to be "man's number" (perhaps counterfeit 777). The worship of a worldwide authority through an image whose defining characteristic is only that it points to "man" is John's interpretation of history. Not only in Nebuchadnezzar's Babylon do saints have to suffer, but the principle of humanity's self-worship is ever-present in time. John writes that the discernment of self-worship (man's number) calls for wisdom (13:18). The Jews who stood up to the king in Babylon were introduced in chapter 1 as wise, and were able to discern the times and understand their opportunity to confess the true God. Although they were subject to hostile powers, in the end they were again favored. Oppression opens opportunities for the saints to show forth the wisdom of God.

MOCKING THE IDOLS

Not only does Daniel 3 show the saints vindicated, but it also puts on display the folly of those who bow to the cultural idols. To illustrate this, please do the following exercise: read out loud Daniel 3:2–18.

What was the experience like? Often, when this passage is read in public, it kindles smiles and chuckles, as yet again one must recite the list of officials or musical instruments. The seemingly endless, redundant, verbose, tedious, superfluous, unnecessarily long, repetitive lists of officials and musical instruments ("iterations of enumerations") are intended to associate the events in the story with mindlessly automatic behavior.

> When humans act as automatons or in an absent-minded manner, they become subjects of comedy. . . . In the same manner, the iteration of enumerations in Daniel 3 is comedic because it serves to expose the mechanistic and thoughtless behavior of the pagan worshippers, of the pagan government bureaucracy in particular, and because it elicits laughter in the process. . . . As soon as the instruments sound, the pagans genuflect *en masse* before a lifeless image without a second thought. In effect, the iteration of enumerations helps to portray those pagans as a version of Pavlov's dog. . . . The comic and absurd mechanistic behavior of the pagans is in stark contrast to the behavior of the three pious Jews.[1]

As the dogs would automatically salivate when Pavlov rang the bell in his famous experiment, or even better, as a robot will spring into action when the power switch is thrown, so the pagans of the whole world mindlessly and automatically perform when the music plays. Pagans behave like lifeless, mindless automatons—and thus they have become like that which they worship. To worship the feat of man makes the worshipper something less than human.

Psalm 135:14–18 reads as follows:

> For the LORD will vindicate his people
>   and have compassion on his servants.
> The idols of the nations are silver and gold,
>   made by the hands of men.
> They have mouths, but cannot speak,
>   eyes, but they cannot see;

they have ears, but cannot hear,
     nor is there breath in their mouths.
Those who make them will be like them,
     and so will all who trust in them.

Those who make them and trust in them will be like them; they will have mouths but be unable to speak, eyes but be unable to see, and so on. I am a worshipper of Nebuchadnezzar's Feat, I am bowing down, bowing down, again and again, the mind not engaged, automatic behavior—I have become a mindless automaton—like the thing I am worshipping. The text says that when Nebuchadnezzar was enraged at the Jews, the *tselem* of his face changed (v. 19). The *tselem* that he set up causes the *tselem* of his face to change—he has become like it.

When the text is read aloud, the reader and audience laugh, because it is written in a silly way—just as idolatry itself is silly. This is how the book of Daniel handles idolatry, rather than with an outright critique. It is simply shown to be ridiculous.

The automatic behavior of the pagans is portrayed almost as an addiction. How many today behave like this with various things, such as alcohol or drugs or pornography? Some bow down automatically before a lifeless thing, forfeiting something alive in themselves. Addictions are a form of idolatry. The addict is in the grip of the idol, and becomes like a robot when engaged in the idolatry.

The alternative to this is to be alive toward God. The Jews standing before the king stand in stark contrast to the pagans. Fully alive, they know their God and are free of the addictive behavior of the pagans. God gives true life, and this life and wisdom enable the saints to stand against societal idolatry in any form, even when threatened with severe repercussions. This is because, in reality, the pagans who worship a lifeless idol are already dead, and the life enjoyed by the worshippers of God cannot really be taken away. So there they stand, at the mercy of the king, prepared to be cast into the fiery furnace.

NEBUCHADNEZZAR'S SELF-IMAGE

> Shadrach, Meshach and Abednego replied to the king, "O Nebuchadnezzar, we do not need to defend ourselves before you in this matter. If we are thrown into the blazing furnace, the God we serve is able to save us from it, and he will rescue us from your hand, O king. But even if he does not, we want you to know, O king, that we will not serve your gods or worship the image of gold you have set up." (Dan. 3:16–18)

The meaning of chapter 3 is that the God whom Israel worships is the true God, despite whatever idol the world presently is bowing down before. Daniel's companions declared that even if they perished in man-made flames, nothing the king could do would compel them to go along with the societal idol. At issue was not what was best for their safety and prosperity. To bow down would ensure their survival; they did not know what God would do. At issue was the truth of the Most High God, which the king admitted in the end (3:28–29). Since they knew the Most High God (as he is called in this chapter), they were able to see through counterfeits. Knowing the genuine article protects one from lies and pseudogods. One who knows the true and living God is not easily swept away with the mindless, automatic idolatry of one's contemporaries.

Nebuchadnezzar acknowledged this in the end. In fact, Nebuchadnezzar seems to be the main character of the story. He is the one who discovers the fourth person in the flames, and he is the one whose mood changes from satisfaction to anger to wonder to praising God. He learns and changes and grows. In the beginning of the chapter, the king is characterized as one who needs universal kudos to be contented. Needing the praise of man, continuous acknowledgement, is the opposite of acknowledging God. It is a never-ending felt need, since in the end there are never enough human accolades on earth to truly satisfy. Another example of this is Haman in the book of Esther; although everyone in Susa bowed down to him, Mordecai wouldn't, and this was intolerable to Haman, inspiring murderous schemes. To live for the approval, respect, or love of others is itself a form of idolatry. The worshippers of Nebuchadnezzar's Feat are reduced to subhuman robots, and the king himself is reduced to a pathetic addict of universal approval. When he doesn't get it, he responds with a temper tantrum.

How much approval do you need to be happy? If someone doesn't like you, or doesn't respect you, or doesn't love you, how does that make you feel? Do you respond with inordinate anger like Nebuchadnezzar? Or perhaps your temper tantrum takes the form of indulging in waves of self-pity, or a pathetic attempt to manipulate others. Nebuchadnezzar needed his own accomplishment to be the object of devotion—but by the end of the story the image is forgotten and the three men, with the son of God, take its place. Knowing the Most High God reveals counterfeits for what they are. The antidote to inordinate anger, or any other idolatrous response to not getting one's own way, is to give up the idol for the sake of God.

> Then Nebuchadnezzar said, "Praise be to the God of Shadrach, Meshach and Abednego, who has sent his angel and rescued his servants! They trusted in him and defied the king's command and were willing to give up their lives rather than serve or worship any god except their own God. Therefore I decree that the people of any nation or language who

say anything against the God of Shadrach, Meshach and Abednego be cut into pieces and their houses be turned into piles of rubble, for no other god can save in this way." (Dan. 3:28–29)

However, even in the decree at the end, we see Nebuchadnezzar taking control of the situation, making the event, again, all about himself. Change is never easy, and giving up one's addiction is difficult. Nebuchadnezzar has to hit rock bottom first, in chapter 4.

THE FIERY FURNACE

What would this story have meant to those suffering at the hands of hostile nations during and after the exile? All of Israel could identify with the three Jews, since the fiery furnace is a metaphor for their captivity. Deuteronomy 4:15–20 warns against idolatry, and concludes, "But as for you, the LORD took you and brought you out of the iron-smelting furnace, out of Egypt, to be the people of his inheritance, as you now are." Egypt was to all Israel what the fiery furnace was to Shadrach, Meshach, and Abednego. Isaiah 43:2 promises that when Israel walks through the fire, they will not be burned.

Death in the Bible is associated with the idea of *consumption*. In Revelation 19:20–21, the birds of carrion, the lake of fire, and the sword consume. In the Old Testament idiom "struck with the edge of the sword," the word "edge" is the Hebrew word "mouth." The sword devours its victim (see also Ezek. 21:28–32). Isaiah 66:24 describes the "worm" and the "fire" as twin sources of everlasting mastication. Sheol and the pit in Ezekiel 32 consume the world.

In Daniel, death also exhibits this quality. In Daniel 3:8 and 6:24, the court officials "ate the pieces of the Jews" (literal translation)—they were tearing into Shadrach,

Meshach, and Abednego like wild beasts. Literal lions were left to ingest Daniel in chapter 6. And in our story of chapter 3, the furnace of blazing fire is a pit which consumes its prey. The heroes did not narrowly escape death in the fiery furnace—they passed the point of no return. They were given up to the consuming flames. Not only did they come to the brink of death, they crossed the line from life to death. They actually fell into the pit. They were lost souls.

But when the king peered into the holocaust, he saw them walking around, and a fourth person who looked like "a son of the gods" with them. Death had no power over them (3:27). They exited the incinerator as if rising from a grave. This is the great reversal of chapter 3, the unexpected turn of events wherein Nebuchadnezzar points away from his image to this God who delivers his faithful worshippers. A similar event is found in chapter 6, where Daniel walks out of the sealed tomb of the lions' den, having passed into the pit of consumption. Again, God supernaturally intervened to bring him back. The motif of deliverance from death reaches its climax in chapter 12, the terminus of the revealed future course of history, with the physical resurrection of every person who ever died, the final Great Reversal at the end of time, when everyone will experience what Shadrach, Meshach, and Abednego did— one like the Son of God will not forsake them even in death and will lead them out of the grave into newness of life. Even the clothing of the three heroes did not stink of death; the inferno had no sting. So it will be with every believer in the Son of God who stands up in faith against the idols of society. Egypt was the furnace for Israel, and the present world is the furnace for the church. All may identify with the three, knowing that the Most High God delivers his people from perdition. The stories of chapters 3 and 6, when the faithful pass into the sphere of death and are brought back, point to the resurrection of all at the end of time.

This final resurrection has already begun. The first one resurrected was Christ, with many soon to follow. Paul calls Christ's resurrection the "firstfruits of those who have fallen asleep" (1 Cor. 15:20–23). Jesus' is the first resurrection, the first of many. So, with Christ, the general resurrection at the end of time has begun.

There is a mysterious way that saints share in Christ's sufferings just as they share in his glory (1 Peter 4:12–17). When Christians around the world suffer for their faith, they are identifying with him in his own passion and death. But the newness of life—the cleansed conscience and peace beyond understanding—is also the property of Christians as they share today, ahead of time, his glory. When we walk through the flames, he is with us; when we suffer, we are comforted.

FOR FURTHER REFLECTION

1. In what do you boast? What makes you inordinately angry? The answer to these questions points to the idolatry in your own heart.
2. What is the point of your accomplishments in this life? How content are you to learn that they will amount to nothing in the end?
3. What is your response to the revelation of God? Do you humble yourself before his sovereignty? Or do you rail against him?
4. Do you need everyone to appreciate you and your works?
5. What did the king call the fourth figure in the fire? Why is that figure there in the fire with the faithful servants of God?

7

NEBUCHADNEZZAR'S STUMP
(INSANITY)

Daniel 4 uses an account of the insanity of King Nebuchadnezzar to highlight the madness of pride and sin. Needing the world to bow before his Feat is deranged. His insanity is recorded to highlight themes of hubris. The one thing moderns should not do is try to psychoanalyze Nebuchadnezzar! Again, this is a mantic dream revelatory of future events, not revelatory of the king's subconscious.

Nebuchadnezzar dreamed of a great tree that gave shelter to the entire world. As he watched, something dreadful happened.

> I saw in the visions of my head as I lay in bed, and behold, a watcher, a holy one, came down from heaven. He cried aloud and said thus, "Hew down the tree and cut off its branches, strip off its leaves and scatter its fruit; let the beasts flee from under it and the birds from its branches. But leave the stump of its roots in the earth, bound with a band of iron and bronze, amid the tender grass of the field. Let

him be wet with the dew of heaven; let his lot be with the beasts in the grass of the earth; let his mind be changed from a man's, and let a beast's mind be given to him; and let seven times pass over him. The sentence is by the decree of the watchers, the decision by the word of the holy ones, to the end that the living may know that the Most High rules the kingdom of men, and gives it to whom he will, and sets over it the lowliest of men." (Dan. 4:13–17 RSV)

Nebuchadnezzar, symbolized by the tree stump, was to lose his human reason and learn the hard way that God prevails over the kingdoms of self-important kings.

PSYCHOANALYZING NEBUCHADNEZZAR

In his *Introduction to the Old Testament*, R. K. Harrison writes:

The illness described in Daniel . . . constitutes a rare form of *monomania*, a condition of mental imbalance in which the sufferer is deranged, in one significant area only. The particular variety of monomania described is known as *boanthropy*, another rare condition in which Nebuchadnezzar imagined himself to be a cow or a bull, and acted accordingly. The European "werewolf" legends are based upon another infrequently encountered form of monomania known as *lycanthropy*. . . . The present writer . . . considers himself particularly fortunate to have actually observed a clinical case of boanthropy in a British mental institution in 1946. . . . Without institutional care the patient would have manifested precisely the same physical conditions as those mentioned in Daniel 4:33.[1]

Perhaps locating the king's malady in a known psychological category makes the story seem more authentic and historical. But Daniel does not divulge if the king had a family history of mental illness, if he abused mind-altering substances, if his head suffered trauma; if the immediate fulfillment means he deteriorated all at once or gradually through the "seven times"; or what treatment if any was offered for this condition beyond ostracism. Most importantly, the text is so selective in what it records that a clinical diagnosis is impossible. That "a beast's mind [was] given to him" is not a scientific description! Perhaps the recorded symptoms were not even the psychologically interesting features of his illness. We cannot know if Harrison's eyewitness account (above) really describes the suffering of Nebuchadnezzar.

Nevertheless, commentators do offer psychological explanations. "Nebuchadnezzar was evidently aware of some degree of guilt which worked itself out, first in the dream and then in delusions."[2] "He was aware in the depths of his being that he had been bestial in his lifestyle. . . . Perhaps through the mechanism of the dream God had shown him what he knew to be true but had consistently repressed from his thoughts."[3] But in the text there is no continuum between suppressed guilt feelings and insanity, but between actual guilt and insanity. The account was not intended for insight into Nebuchadnezzar's repressed feelings, but rather to show how God felt about Nebuchadnezzar. Nebuchadnezzar's being given the mind of a beast is a judgment of God for his hubris and oppression of the poor. The specifics of the mode of lunacy are secondary in the passage to the overall theme of pride and to the literary motif of the beast. These concerns will be treated below.

There is a continuum, impossible to miss, between the king's proud words and the pronouncement of his doom.

He said, "Is not this the great Babylon I have built as the royal residence, by my mighty power and for the glory of my majesty?"

The words were still on his lips when a voice came from heaven, "This is what is decreed for you, King Nebuchadnezzar: Your royal authority has been taken from you. You will be driven away from people and will live with the wild animals; you will eat grass like cattle. Seven times will pass by for you until you acknowledge that the Most High is sovereign over the kingdoms of men and gives them to anyone he wishes." (Dan. 4:30–32)

The arrogance of the king provoked God to strike him with an extraordinary dementia. His self-exalting spirit necessitated this judgment. To save him from this doom Daniel pled with him to turn from oppressing the poor.

In the Bible, insanity is variously associated with pride and willful rebellion against God—and therefore, of course, against reality. The prodigal son "came to his senses" in Luke 15:17; previously he was not himself. He was dissociated from his true condition until he came to his senses and returned in humility to the father he had insulted and disparaged. In Romans 1 God gave idolaters up to a depraved mind, to futile thinking. Foolish idolatry leads to disintegration, perversion, and finally death. Exchanging the truth for a lie, living not in reality but in a delusion, idolaters have given up reality to worship images of beasts.

There was a man bound in chains who broke them and hid naked in a graveyard, with not a single mental disease but legion. Clearly insane, he had a spiritual problem—he needed to be freed from demonic possession (Luke 8). Here is a direct biblical link between the symptoms of chronic schizophrenia and being in the grip of the forces of darkness. John 9 draws an analogy between the literally blind man and the willfully blind leaders who refuse to face reality and so persecute the one touched by Jesus.

> Jesus said, "For judgment I have come into this world, so that the blind will see and those who see will become blind." Some Pharisees who were with him heard him say this and asked, "What? Are we blind too?" Jesus said, "If you were blind, you would not be guilty of sin; but now that you claim you can see, your guilt remains." (John 9:39–41)

All sin is insanity; nothing is more bizarre than sin. Why would anyone build his house on sand? Or choose a path, knowing it leads to death? In this sense, any person who sins is disconnected from reality and not completely sane. In Nebuchadnezzar's case, his delusional state is seen in his exploitation of the poor (Dan. 4:27). He saw himself at the center of all things, demanding that every creature worship his handiwork, in direct opposition to the revelation of God in chapter 2! A direct biblical link is discovered between a depraved mind and a diseased one. Before the judgment fell, Daniel sought to avert disaster by calling upon the king to repent of his evil ways. Daniel tried to liberate Nebuchadnezzar from his *moral* insanity before it was too late—before the tree was cut down and the pending judgment fell. Repentance was the real cure, the way to true sanity.

However, the spiritual condition of the king did not change—he did not listen to the advice of his counselor—and he passed beyond rational appeal into a psychopathic state of mind. The moral or spiritual insanity of pride and sin (which is common to every sinner) was judged by the imposition of another kind. The mind of a man was changed into the mind of a beast (4:16). At this point, the time for repentance was over. No therapy would have been effective. There was no receptive human heart left—there was only a bestial center. Previously, the king had been unwilling to heed Daniel's counsel; now he became unable to respond until the "seven times" were completed.

In Romans 1 God gave up idolaters to a depraved mind, abandoning them to depraved behavior, which was "the due penalty for their perversion" (Rom. 1:27). Deuteronomy 28:28–29 also speaks of God's judgments of blinding madness for rebellion. Nebuchadnezzar, while insane, was driven out from human comforts and lived like an animal. At this point, the opportunity to respond to God's warnings was past.

This could have been averted. God and Daniel warned the king that his evil ways must change. Long before the judgment fell, the king was in great danger—yet no one would warn him of it except Daniel. On the roof of his palace, Nebuchadnezzar's state of mind was one of great self-esteem. He was a model success story, surrounded by sycophants who were more than willing to bow before his Feat. Standing there, he bragged, "Is not this the great Babylon I have built as the royal residence, by my mighty power and for the glory of my majesty?" Would any psychologist at that point have diagnosed him with monomania? He was the model of mental health! But Daniel discerned a spiritual problem that if unchecked would inevitably lead to catastrophe.

Daniel was not happy that the king would finally get his comeuppance. God's righteous decrees would prevail, but in a manner that gave Daniel no pleasure. He was troubled and tried to save the king. This is like evangelizing a non-Christian. Daniel pled with him to turn from his self-trust and self-aggrandizement to acknowledging that God is sovereign. Nebuchadnezzar conceptualized his own works as a false god (chap. 3). He needed to turn from this to serve God and the eternal kingdom—the Rock not made with human hands that would grow and fill the earth. Christians can see in this a model of how to preach the gospel—call the unbeliever from false conceptions to the Most High God. But Nebuchadnezzar had to hit rock bottom before he changed, and lived like an animal for seven years.

What is mental health? What is normal? The question is problematic. Sanity might be defined in terms of what is helpful as opposed to what is harmful, or perhaps by the behavior of the majority. Some might label Christian self-sacrificial love "codependency"; Freud called religion the "universal neurosis"; homosexuality is called normal; alcoholism, a disease. So what is sane?

> At the end of that time, I, Nebuchadnezzar, raised my eyes toward heaven, and my sanity was restored. Then I praised the Most High; I honored and glorified him who lives forever. . . . Now I, Nebuchadnezzar, praise and exalt and glorify the King of heaven, because everything he does is right and all his ways are just. And those who walk in pride he is able to humble. (Dan. 4:34, 37)

"Sanity was restored" when Nebuchadnezzar acknowledged his pride and looked away from himself to the sovereign God. Just as there was a strong connection between his boasting and insanity, so there is between lifting one's eyes to heaven and sanity. Joyce Baldwin comments, "It is important to note the connection here between the exercise of faith and the return of reason. While he was full of his own importance Nebuchadnezzar's world revolved around himself. It did not strike him how unrealistic this was until he was brought low by illness. Sanity begins with realistic self-appraisal."[4]

Sanity begins not only with a "realistic self-appraisal" but also, of course, with a realistic God-appraisal. To acknowledge that only the sovereign God's kingdom is eternal is sanity. To place one's own kingdom as first in importance is insane. As Jesus told his disciples, "If any man would come after me, let him deny himself and take up his cross and follow me. For whoever would save his life will lose it, and whoever loses his life for my sake will find it" (Matt. 16:24–25 RSV).

To be a disciple of Jesus one must be willing to let go of one's own life, to repent of what seems most valuable, to give up the idea of being the captain of one's own ship. It is to lift up one's eyes—to the cross—and to see there one's own identity. To become a Christian is to become sane, to embrace reality, to know the true and living God. It is to cease putting oneself first and rejoice in God's gracious way of being able to humble anyone—including you. You are called as well to turn from your own sins, lest you rouse God to extraordinary action to bring you to the point of saying with Nebuchadnezzar, "All his ways are just. And those who walk in pride he is able to humble."

THE DREAM-TREE

I said, "Belteshazzar, chief of the magicians, I know that the spirit of the holy gods is in you, and no mystery is too difficult for you. Here is my dream; interpret it for me. These are the visions I saw while lying in my bed: I looked, and there before me stood a tree in the middle of the land. Its height was enormous. The tree grew large and strong and its top touched the sky; it was visible to the ends of the earth. Its leaves were beautiful, its fruit abundant, and on it was food for all. Under it the beasts of the field found shelter, and the birds of the air lived in its branches; from it every creature was fed." (Dan. 4:9–12)

And the interpretation:

The tree you saw, which grew large and strong, with its top touching the sky, visible to the whole earth, with beautiful leaves and abundant fruit, providing food for all, giving shelter to the beasts of the field, and having nesting places in its branches for the birds of the air—you, O king, are that tree! You have become great and strong; your greatness has grown until it reaches the sky, and your dominion extends to distant parts of the earth. (Dan. 4:20–22)

As the head of gold stood for both Nebuchadnezzar and his kingdom, the tree of this dream also stands for both. It is Babylon in all its beauty, strength, geographical extent, and especially in its capacity to care for its subjects.

Jesus refers to Daniel a number of times in the Gospels. He takes the Rock of Daniel 2 that grows to fill the earth as a reference to himself (Luke 20:14–19). His words are the Rock to build one's life upon (Matt. 7:24–27). Paul calls Jesus the Rock (Rom. 9:30–33). In Daniel 7:13–22, the son of man approaches the Ancient of Days; Jesus claims that this speaks of himself (Matt. 26:63–64).

In a similar way, in a parable Jesus uses imagery from Daniel to describe the kingdom of God: "The kingdom of heaven is like a mustard seed, which a man took and planted in his field. Though it is the smallest of all your seeds, yet when it grows, it is the largest of garden plants and becomes a tree, so that the birds of the air come and perch in its branches" (Matt. 13:31–32). Here we have the image of a tree representing the kingdom of God, growing to fill the earth and shelter the world (Dan. 4:11). In the dream-tree, the birds of the air and beasts of the field represent those who find rest in Nebuchadnezzar's kingdom. By analogy, the birds in the branches of the kingdom represent those who have rested in Christ and found shelter under another tree—the cross. The kingdom grows and grows until it shelters the whole earth, just as the Rock of Daniel 2 filled the earth.[5]

The dream-tree was cut down and became a stump. The stump was the tree bereft of beauty and power, Nebuchadnezzar reduced to a bestial existence. One can no more find a known psychosis in Nebuchadnezzar's lunacy than one can diagnose him from the description of the stump. But if the description of his insanity is not amenable to psychological analysis, then why is it given? What is the point of recording the particularities of his monomania?

The king in his pride was bestial before God. His rule was subhuman, like a wild beast. He was not merely prideful and insane, but terrifying and brutal. The Psalmist confesses that in his ignorance he was a beast (behemoth) before God (Ps. 73:21–22). A wealthy man without knowledge is like beasts that perish (Ps. 49:20). God tests people to demonstrate that they are only beasts, sharing a common fate (Eccl. 3:18–21). Second Peter 2:9–12 describes those who arrogantly blaspheme angels (see Dan. 4:17) as "brute beasts, creatures of instinct, born only to be caught and destroyed, and like beasts they too will perish."

Nebuchadnezzar was such a man. He was a beast before God. God tested him to demonstrate he was only a beast. Like a beast, he and his kingdom would perish. His hair "grew"—using the word earlier translated "great" to describe him. His hair was like eagle's wings, his nails a bird's claws. He ate grass like an ox. In chapter 7 Babylon is described as a lion with eagle's wings that was given the heart of a man. Nebuchadnezzar's kingdom and personal life were beast-like—as reflected in his psychopathic traits. This is part and parcel of the book's beast motif, which climaxes with the lions' den, but continues in subsequent chapters to describe great earthly powers as beasts.

What an insight into the way God sees human society! The great Babylon, sheltering the world, the golden head, had at its heart a subhuman monster. Only the oppressed saints (seen in the person of Daniel) have wisdom to speak the truth of God, but are ignored, though finally vindicated. The great king, his experience interpreted by an evangelist, finally confesses the sovereign God. This is a very different outcome from the next episode; there all that remains for the blasphemous king is judgment and death.

The book of Revelation also portrays human society as a massive worldwide government with a monster at its heart, hell-bent on destroying the saints, who oppose the beast and worship the Lamb (Rev. 13–14). There, an angel sings out, "Fallen, fallen is Babylon the Great!" Then one "like a son of man" reaps the last harvest with a sickle.

The Babylon of Daniel is the world of today and the world of the end time. Saints will be oppressed, but will continue in their testimony to Jesus, come what may. In the end, they will be vindicated.

FOR FURTHER REFLECTION

1. What is reality? If insanity is failure to live according to reality, then who is insane? Is it sane to sin?
2. When should a Christian warn a sinner? Give an example from your own life experience of how this has worked out.
3. God dealt harshly with the contented and prosperous king. When has God been harsh with you to wake you up to your need for him?
4. What is the great tree today that Jesus talks about, that shelters the world? From what are you sheltered?

8

THE HANDWRITING

ON THE WALL

A s noted earlier, A. Lenglet's outline of the Aramaic portion of Daniel shows a chiastic structure (see figure 5).[1] According to this analysis, Daniel 5 should parallel chapter 4. In chapter 4, Nebuchadnezzar dreamed about the great tree that fell; he was then struck with insanity for seven years before being restored and praising God. How can this be parallel to chapter 5, where Belshazzar the king blasphemes God by profaning his temple's vessels, fingers appear with an oracle of doom, and then Belshazzar dies?

Figure 5
The Chiastic Structure of Daniel 2–7

A   Dream statue representing four kingdoms (chap. 2)
  B Worship the golden statue or perish in a pit (chap. 3)
    C Judgment on Nebuchadnezzar (chap. 4)
    C Judgment on Belshazzar (chap. 5)
  B Worship Darius or perish in a pit (chap. 6)
A   Dream of four beasts representing four kingdoms (chap. 7)

There are, in fact, striking similarities between the accounts. Both depict proud Babylonian kings claiming what is proper only to God. These are the only two Babylonian kings met in Daniel. Both receive supernatural warnings of their precarious situations. Both employ Daniel to interpret the meaning of the revelation, who explains that judgment is about to fall and the kingdom is about to be lost. The judgment falls as predicted. John Calvin argues that there is a sort of insanity in chapter 5: "Their madness was the more kindled when they were roused by the heat of wine."[2] The king and his minions were out of their minds with drink, and thus dementedly desecrated the holy objects.

When Daniel speaks to Belshazzar, he specifically refers to chapter 4; Daniel weighs and measures Belshazzar against Nebuchadnezzar and finds him wanting. Belshazzar seems embarrassed at having to seek aid from Daniel and refuses to call him by the name Nebuchadnezzar gave him; upon Daniel's entrance, the king sneers that he is just a captive (5:13). Perhaps Belshazzar is seeking parity with Nebuchadnezzar, so he eschews seeking counsel from the previous court. He offers great gifts to Daniel for help, but Daniel spurns him. The animosity between them is palpable.

MENE MENE TEQEL PARSIN

Fingers mysteriously appear and write a message on the wall. This is analogous to God's communicating through dreams, and a good example of why psychological explanations should be avoided.[3] God supplies the mystery, and then Daniel provides the interpretation. The message was, *Mene, Mene, Teqel,* and *Parsin. Mene* means "to count, number, reckon, assign." It can be vocalized as "mina," a weight worth sixty units or shekels. The word also sounds something like "Mede." *Teqel* means "to weigh" and is the Aramaic cognate to the Hebrew word "shekel," a weight of one unit. *Parsin* or *Peres* means "divide" and sounds like "Persia." It corresponds to a half-weight.

The meaning of a text has at least three loci: the author's intent, the text itself, and the response of the reader. An analogy might be how a computer prints a page. It must send good data to the printer. The printer must understand the protocols sent. And the cable that connects them must be functional. If the author is incompetent, communication cannot take place. If the reader is unreceptive or unintelligent, there is no conveyance of meaning. And if the medium, the text itself (the printer cable in our analogy), is flawed, the message is not understood. All three must work together for meaning to be conveyed; this is the hermeneutical system. The Christian doctrine of the Trinity corresponds with this: the Father is the originator speaking the word, the Son is the Word—the message, and the Spirit interprets for the reader.

A parable tells of a farmer who, while plowing in his field, saw clouds form the letters "PC." He told his pastor, who concluded that the letters meant, "Preach Christ!" So the man dutifully enrolled in seminary, but he did poorly and soon found himself on academic probation. He told the dean about the clouds, who concluded the message meant, "Plant Corn!" When any text is read, there are unanswered questions that naturally arise, gaps in what the author wrote. When gaps are encountered, readers must fill them. For example, where was Daniel in chapter 3? Who was the angel that spent the night with Daniel in chapter 6? These are gaps in the story. When a reader fills in these gaps by theorizing an answer, the reader is engaging in the production of meaning. This is one way to understand reader response as a locus of meaning. The Holy Spirit interprets as a reader reads actively and is engaged in the production of meaning, along with the author and the text itself.

Sometimes one brings one's *pesher* to the *raz*. The meaning in the case of the clouds of our parable does not really reside in the clouds, but in the interpreter. In chapter 5, Daniel is not so much explaining what secret meaning is encrypted in the four words on the wall as he is providing an explanation that fits. The writing on the wall is nothing but gaps. It is so esoteric that the meaning is generated almost entirely by the godly and gifted interpreter.

Why couldn't the wise men read the handwriting on the wall?[4] Aramaic was the common language of the empire; why would they need someone to read it? It is as if they couldn't recognize the actual words on the wall. Why was *Mene* repeated? In the old Greek translation of Daniel, *Mene* occurs only once. In Daniel 5:5, "fingers" write. It is easy to extend one's index finger to trace out words in plaster. But can anyone write a word such as *Mene* using multiple fingers at once? It cannot be done. Yet the text seems to indicate that fingers appeared and made undecipherable scratches on the wall that Daniel read as words.

Ancient Babylon used a sexagesimal (base-60) numbering system. In the base-10 system, a single stroke, "1", can stand for 1, and 10, and 100, and so on. The difference in value is denoted by where the stroke is positioned, the position indicated by zeros. In a base-60 system, a single stroke, |, also indicates 1, but in the next position it indicates not 10 but 60. Two strokes then, ||, would indicate 61; the first stroke is 60, and the second is 1.

A single stroke, representing the number 1, corresponds to a unit weight, or a teqel. But it could also correspond to a 60-unit weight, or a mina. Three strokes, |||, might be three minas, three teqels, two minas and a teqel, or two teqels and a mina. Perhaps a stroke with a line through it, +, could be half a weight; call it a peresh. So these markings, ||| +, could be read "Mina, Mina, Teqel, Peresh," with a value of 121 1/2. "Mina" sounds like the verb *mene*, "to number," and it also sounds like "Medes." "Teqel" sounds like the verb *taqal*, "to weigh." "Peresh" sounds like the verb *parash*, "to divide," and it also sounds like "Persia."

David Brewer suggests that a hand appeared, with its four fingers and thumb spread out, and then drew together into a fist, scratching the plaster with a sign that looked like ||| + . (Of course, Daniel was free to read it right to left if he wanted [like Hebrew or Aramaic script], in which case it would appear as + |||. This would make the hand's owner right-handed.) None of the Magi could explain the scratches, until Daniel was called. He looked at the markings and formulated his *pesher*. He read the first two strokes as being 60 weights (minas) apiece, and used the verb *mene*, "to number"—God has numbered Belshazzar's days and ended them! The next single stroke he read as a teqel, "to weigh"—the king was weighed and found wanting! A peresh could be formed by the index finger crossing the thumb, creating a + sign (a teqel divided in half), *parash*, "to divide"—the kingdom is divided and given to the Medes and Persians! In other words, to paraphrase, Daniel looked at the pathologically terrified king who wanted to know the meaning of the scratches, and he said in effect, "You want to know what they mean? You're going to die, you're going to die, and you're going to die! That's what they mean, you evil king!"

In this interpretation the number that Daniel read in the scratches was 121 1/2 (two minas worth 60 each, a teqel worth 1, and a half weight). But Brewer points out that there are other ways they might have been read. Three teqels and a peresh would yield 3 1/2, or "a time, times, and half a time," half of 7. Three and a half years is 42 months, with 1,260 days (each month having 30 days and each year 360). These time periods occur elsewhere in Daniel (7:25; 12:7) and Revelation (11:2–3; 12:6; 12:14; 13:5).

In another interpretation, one mina, two teqels, and a peresh would be 62 1/2. In Daniel 9:23–27, 70 weeks of years are predicted before the end. These are divided into periods of 62 weeks, 7 weeks, and two halves of one week. Attaching one half of one week to the 62 yields 62 1/2 weeks as part of the unfolding 70 weeks of years. Of course, the other half week of years is 3 1/2 years. Thus the scratches made by fingers in the wall spun out a numerology that governs the course of apocalyptic history. The eschatological series of events is set according to a calendar that is controlled by these marks. The numbers 3 1/2, 7, and 62 1/2 are used in the construction of the stages of the end times in Daniel and Revelation.

What is the interpretation? What does the writing mean? It means that in the course of eschatological history the dream of Nebuchadnezzar is about to be fulfilled and the age of the golden head will pass into the age of the silver chest; the lion of Daniel's dream (chap. 7) is about to be eaten by the bear. It means that there will be 70 weeks of years between the anointed Cyrus and the anointed coming king, divided into 7, halves of 7, and 62 1/2. It means that the saints must endure (Dan. 7:25) and the woman be protected (Rev. 12:14) for a time, times, and half a time. It means that for 42 months the Gentiles will trample the holy city (Rev. 11:2). The eschatological course of apocalyptic history is seen in scratches made before the eyes of the pagan Belshazzar, and interpreted for him by the faithful Belteshazzar.

Perhaps this may help in interpreting apocalyptic. Like the scratches on the wall, apocalyptic dreams and visions are very esoteric and cryptically symbolic, such that one has to know the answer before one interprets. Daniel 11, for example, could not have been used to predict the future before the events happened, but after the fact one may see the historical events reflected there—interpretation *ex eventu*.

The writing on Belshazzar's wall was a word of judgment. Along with tying these markings together with future history, it is also possible to see them as definitive for the state of fallen humanity before a holy God. Kim Monroe argues that all human beings might have such a warning written on their own walls—weighed and found wanting, numbered days, kingdom lost.[5] Only one person would have something different on his wall: weighed and found worthy of unnumbered days and an eternal kingdom. This person is Jesus. Monroe points out that now what is properly on Jesus' wall is written on Christians' walls as well, and what is properly written on Christians' walls is found on his—he is weighed and found wanting on our behalf so that when we are weighed, we are found worthy because he is worthy.

MOCKING THE IDOLS

There are parallels between chapters 3 and 5 of Daniel. Belshazzar made a feast, and Nebuchadnezzar made an image, to solidify power and secure the kingdom in the face of the obvious fact of its inevitable fall. "Belshazzar's banquet was sheer bravado, the last fling of a terrified ruler unsuccessfully attempting to drown his fears."[6] As the idol was mocked in chapter 3 through the "iterations of enumerations," so here the gods worshipped by Belshazzar and his guests are not named, but called several times "gods of gold and silver, bronze, iron, wood and stone." The redundant list of building materials underscores the lifeless and artificial quality of the so-called gods they worshipped. Again, needless repetition of this sort has the effect of making the faceless, nameless, artificial, anonymous, stone-cold-dead, impotent gods appear absurd.

There is another way idols and idolaters are mocked in chapter 5.[7] When the evil king saw the fingers, the text says that the "knots" (*qetar*) of his loins were "loosened" (*shera'*) (5:6). The Authorized Version reads, "the joints of his loins were loosed." This is translated variously, for example, "his limbs gave way" (RSV) or "his legs gave way beneath him" (NLT). But it is specifically the knots of his *loins* that were loosened, which might be an image of losing sphincter control—incontinence. In this way the text pokes fun at the blasphemous king. He who sought power over Yahweh's bowls could not control his own bowels!

The queen mother then informed the king of one who could "solve" (*shera'*) "puzzles" (*qetar*) (5:12). Daniel, in a sense, was in the same position as Yahweh's vessels—a captive of Babylon, and set apart with them as pure (1:2–4). Notice the wordplay in the queen mother's remarks—she knows of one who can loosen the king's knots for him! When Daniel appears finally before him, the king says, "I understand you can solve [*shera'*] puzzles [*qetar*]" (5:16)! Al Wolters writes,

> We must look at the story from the point of view of an Aramaic-speaking Israelite who had suffered much at the hands of the Babylonians. The Babylonian king is described as first insulting the Israelite God and then, when the latter responds with the mysterious handwriting on the wall, as being so frightened that the "knots of his loins were untied." This ignominious spectacle is enough to elicit hoots of derisive laughter on the part of the audience. After the pagan wise men have failed to interpret the riddle, the queen mother recommends the Israelite prophet Daniel, whom she describes to the king as particularly competent to "untie knots" for him [5:12]. The unwitting *double entendre* evokes more derisive laughter. Finally, the king himself comes face to face with Daniel . . . and says, in effect, "I understand that you can untie my knots for me" [5:16]. Again we imagine the audience's uproarious laughter as the hapless pagan king unwittingly makes a fool of himself before the prophet of the

Lord. We see how the story uses burlesque humor to underscore the sovereignty of the Israelite God, before whom the great kings of the earth can at a moment's notice be reduced to figures of fun, preparatory to being brought to justice.[8]

There can be no danger from these idols, they are just silly. And they certainly did not save the king from his doom. Sometimes mocking the idols of our own time or in our own personal lives is an important part of being set free from them. Ridiculing the ridiculous is a serious apologetics technique. For example, pointing out the silliness of attempts to explain away the resurrection, exposing the fact that it takes more faith to believe that life arose by chance than by a Creator, highlighting the illogic of rejecting Christ but valuing Christian virtues, are all effective polemics. Also, counseling one who is feeling unappreciated by pushing the feeling to an absurd extreme ("I want them all to bow down when I walk in the room, to say, 'You are the greatest ever'—I want every person on earth to love and respect me") sometimes can expose the irrational heart and set it free from unrealistic expectations.

Like the temple vessels and the captive Jews, Christians are set apart by God. He will not permit his church to be persecuted and abused forever. There comes a time when arrogant powers are weighed and found lacking. Their days are numbered. Their kingdom will be, in the end, divided and inherited by the saints (7:18). In the meantime, the ability to laugh at the absurdity of the world's idols helps us to see through its grand claims.

GENERAL REVELATION

Daniel was called because the pagan advisors could not interpret the word of God (5:8). All their skills in other fields of knowledge were useless to help the terrorized king. But these skills had been designed to make them wise in just this kind of situation. They were supposed to be able to interpret signs and portents and advise the king on great decisions. Yet all of their wisdom was futile to aid the pale and knee-knocking king.

General revelation is what God reveals concerning himself in all things, a revelation to which every person has some access. Paul argues that God plainly reveals that there is a Supreme Being, and this knowledge renders all without excuse in the judgment that is coming when they are weighed and found wanting.

> The wrath of God is being revealed from heaven against all the godlessness and wickedness of men who suppress the truth by their wickedness, since what may be known about God is plain to them, because God has made it plain to them. For since the creation of the world God's invisible qualities— his eternal power and divine nature—have been clearly seen, being understood from what has been made, so that men are without excuse.
>
> For although they knew God, they neither glorified him as God nor gave thanks to him, but their thinking became futile and their foolish hearts were darkened. Although they claimed to be wise, they became fools and exchanged the glory of the immortal God for images made to look like mortal man and birds and animals and reptiles. Therefore God gave them over in the sinful desires of their hearts to sexual impurity for the degrading of their bodies with one another. They exchanged the truth of God for a lie, and worshiped and served created things rather than the Creator—who is forever praised. Amen. (Rom. 1:18–25)

It is not that God reveals facts such as the laws of physics. Rather, it is that the laws of physics reveal something about God that carries authority, to which every physicist must respond either in faith or unbelief. Pagans know the true God on some level but self-consciously suppress this knowledge; this is the universal neurosis. Worshipping beasts, they degrade themselves. An atheist learns many facts—how things work, what equations govern gravity—but he cannot learn what is true about God that is being revealed through those equations.

In the same way, those unable to understand the word of God on the wall were also unable to understand what God revealed in history. Belshazzar, Daniel accused, should have known by his own family history not to trifle with God (5:22). The lessons of general revelation did not move him to honor God, but served only to render him without excuse. In the same way, the brilliance of non-Christian scientists, politicians, and scholars will in the end serve only to render them without excuse, since "God's invisible qualities— his eternal power and divine nature—have been clearly seen, being understood from what has been made, so that men are without excuse. For although they knew God, they neither glorified him as God nor gave thanks to him."

This has far-reaching evangelistic and apologetic ramifications. Christians able to interpret God's word are also able to understand the revelation of God in every field of knowledge. Christians can thus proclaim the gospel of Christ using every fact ever discovered. Daniel did not just argue from the word of God as written—he also argued from general knowledge, and so can every Christian.

FOR FURTHER REFLECTION

1. Was Belshazzar sane? Why or why not?
2. What are some of the idols of our age? Describe ways to mock these idols—to highlight their absurdity.

3. Belshazzar blasphemed God's sacred objects—what form does blasphemy take today?
4. Do people learn from history? What use is general revelation? How can this knowledge be used in evangelism?
5. What word do you deserve to have written on your wall? Because of Jesus, what is written there instead?

9

WORSHIPPING MAN

Daniel 3 and 6 are parallel. In both, sovereigns demand that the world worship them, and when Jews refuse to do so, they are cast (*remah*, "cast"— same word in both chapters) into a pit. In chapter 3, the three Jews were thrown into the pit of fire; in chapter 6, Daniel is abandoned in a pit of lions. In both cases, the victims to be devoured were saved through angelic intervention.

King Darius's officials were jealous of Daniel, but could find no fault with him. Daniel's one trait they could exploit was his religion, and he allowed himself to be manipulated rather than hide his devotion to the living God. Daniel 6:24 calls Daniel's accusers those "who ate his pieces." They were the human equivalent to the lions themselves—those who sought to devour the saints.

The set-up was that for a period of thirty days, all citizens were to pray only to Darius. But Daniel prayed to his God as he always did—publicly—and was arrested. Darius could find no legal way to save him, so Daniel was thrown into the den of lions. There, an angel shut the lions' mouths. Daniel emerged safely, and his accusers were thrown in with their families, who were immediately mauled and broken. The worship of Darius was forgotten, and Darius himself praised the living God.

IDOLATRY

The book of Daniel treats idolatry differently than elsewhere in Scripture. No false god is named in Daniel. In chapter 3, what was worshipped was Nebuchadnezzar's magnificent work, which was not even a religious object. This is a picture of a culture bowing down to a human accomplishment. Nebuchadnezzar was really the idol; man was being worshipped and rivaled God. When the Jews were accused, the charge was that they "pay no attention to you, O king. They neither serve your gods nor worship the image of gold you have set up" (3:12). The gods of the king took second place to his image. (The accusation was not, "They pay no attention to the gods.") Idolatry was universal, institutional, and dangerous for anyone who refused to comply. Enforcement against rejecting the culture's ideology was swift and terrible. In chapter 4, Nebuchadnezzar claimed the glory and majesty of the city of Babylon for himself, but in the end he was forced to acknowledge that God rules, not the king. In chapter 5, Belshazzar worships idols, but none are named. They have no identity because they are not real—the genuine objects of worship are not gods, but kingdoms and kings. In chapter 6, again a divine being is not in view. This brings the earlier chapters into crystal-clear focus. For a period of thirty days, the worship of a man is to be observed to the exclusion of the worship of any god.

One might expect that being worshipped as a god by all the people would be a satisfying and exhilarating experience for the king. Nothing is further from the truth! The godlike law of the Medes and Persians (which could not be changed) put Darius in a double bind and served only to reveal that he, the worshipped man, was powerless to save his friend. Darius gets nothing but anxiety and insomnia for all of his divine status. As with Nebuchadnezzar's insanity, when the arrogance of Darius reaches its zenith, he is exposed as impotent.

Idolatry is sometimes treated in the Bible as something nonreligious, not as something directed toward a god but as trusting in something very much of this world. For example, the book of Habakkuk says of the Chaldeans that they are "guilty men, whose own strength is their god" (1:11). The Chaldean "sacrifices to his net and burns incense to his dragnet, for by his net he lives in luxury and enjoys the choicest food" (1:16). Here the Babylonians' true god is identified as themselves, their own strength. The dragnet is a symbol of their instruments of war—the tools of the trade—by which they trap peoples. These people had a religion—their own strength—and to their tools of war they metaphorically "burn incense." They are a people whose religion is their own abilities and means of production. To a modern reader, this might sound like a description of today's world.

Ezekiel spoke to Daniel's contemporaries—those who also were exiles in Babylon. He accused the exiled Jews of idolatry.

> Then came certain of the elders of Israel to me, and sat before me. And the word of the LORD came to me, "Son of man, these men have taken their idols into their hearts, and set the stumbling block of their iniquity before their faces; should I let myself be inquired of at all by them? Therefore speak to them, and say to them, Thus says the Lord GOD: Any man of the house of Israel who takes his idols into his heart and sets the stumbling block of his iniquity before his face, and yet comes to the prophet, I the LORD will answer him myself because of the multitude of his

idols, that I may lay hold of the hearts of the house of Israel, who are all estranged from me through their idols." (Ezek. 14:1–5 RSV)

God told Ezekiel that the Jews had set up idols in their hearts. These are not wood and stone idols. God sees into the human heart, and there he finds idols. Idolatry is internalized. It is an attitude of arrogance and self-reliance (1 Sam. 15:23).

Paul says of the enemies of Christ, "their god is the belly" (Phil. 3:18–21 RSV). Those motivated by sensual pleasure or simply by their next meal worship the god of their belly. Paul contrasts this idolatry with setting one's mind on Christ and citizenship in heaven. Compared to the "surpassing worth of knowing Christ" all things of this world—things that function as people's gods—are refuse (Phil. 3:7–8 RSV). Paul lists a number of "earthly" vices that are not suitable for a Christian, and among these is "covetousness, which is idolatry" (Col. 3:5 RSV). The tenth commandment is not to covet anything that belongs to one's neighbor, including house, spouse, and possessions. All such coveting is called idolatry. To covet is to worship. To know what a person covets is to know that person's god. Greed reveals a discontented heart that believes blessing will be found by securing what is coveted. A person trusts that some thing is able to bless with happiness or peace or comfort, and so chases it as if it were divine and able to bless with life. Jesus contrasts worshipping God with money and says that no one can serve (or worship) two masters (Matt. 6:24). Jesus treats money as rivaling God, as that which can be served as an alternative to God.

Usually in the Old Testament, idolatry is an external religious act of bowing before a wood or stone idol. In the New Testament this is internalized. Boasting in anything, trusting in anything, serving, coveting, are idolatries of the heart—chasing after another god. In Daniel, idolatry always involves nationalism and human pride, never a named deity that competes with Yahweh. There is no hint that the exiles were seduced by Marduk or Bel or other Babylonian gods. But examples abound of the other, deeper kind of idolatry. To know what a person boasts about (such as his Feat) is to know the person's god. To know what provokes inordinate anger (such as when that Feat is spurned) is to know the person's god. To know what places a person in a double bind and creates unbearable anxiety and loss of sleep is to know the person's god.

The text asks the reader, what competes with God in your heart? In what do you boast? Your accomplishments? Your successes? Having the right answers (like the wise men of Babylon)? Having a high position? The book of Daniel shows there is no difference between pride and false worship, between avarice and idolatry, craving delicacies and bowing the knee to wood and stone.

HUMANISM

The twentieth century brought new clarity to the worship of man. The following are quotes of a number of affirmations from the 1933 document, the *Humanist Manifesto*.

The time has come for widespread recognition of the radical changes in religious beliefs throughout the modern world. The time is past for mere revision of traditional attitudes. Science and economic change have disrupted the old beliefs. Religions the world over are under the necessity of coming to terms with new conditions created by a vastly increased knowledge and experience. In every field of human activity, the vital movement is now in the direction of a candid and explicit humanism. In order that religious humanism may be better understood we, the undersigned, desire to make certain affirmations which we believe the facts of our contemporary life demonstrate.

FIRST: Religious humanists regard the universe as self-existing and not created.

SECOND: Humanism believes that man is a part of nature and that he has emerged as a result of a continuous process. . . .

EIGHTH: Religious Humanism considers the complete realization of human personality to be the end of man's life and seeks its development and fulfillment in the here and now. This is the explanation of the humanist's social passion.

NINTH: In the place of the old attitudes involved in worship and prayer the humanist finds his religious emotions expressed in a heightened sense of personal life and in a cooperative effort to promote social well-being.

In 1973 the *Humanist Manifesto II* was published. Following are several selections from it:

As in 1933, humanists still believe that traditional theism, especially faith in the prayer-hearing God, assumed to live and care for persons, to hear and understand their prayers, and to be able to do something about them, is an unproved and outmoded faith. Salvationism, based on mere affirmation, still appears as harmful, diverting people with false hopes of heaven hereafter. Reasonable minds look to other means for survival. We believe, however, that traditional dogmatic or authoritarian religions that place revelation, God, ritual, or creed above human needs and experience do a disservice to the human species. Any account of nature should pass the tests of scientific evidence; in our judgment, the dogmas and myths of traditional religions do not do so. Even at this late date in human history, certain elementary facts based upon the critical use of scientific reason have to be restated. We find insufficient evidence for belief in the existence of a supernatural; it is either meaningless or irrelevant to the question of survival and fulfillment of the human race. As nontheists, we begin with humans not God, nature not deity. Nature may indeed be broader and deeper than we now know; any new discoveries, however, will but enlarge our knowledge of the natural.

But we can discover no divine purpose or providence for the human species. While there is much that we do not know, humans are responsible for what we are or will become. No deity will save us; we must save ourselves.

SECOND: Promises of immortal salvation [and] fear of eternal damnation are both illusory and harmful. They distract humans from present concerns, from self-actualization, and from rectifying social injustices. Modern science discredits such historic concepts as the "ghost in the machine" and the "separable soul." Rather, science affirms that the human species is an emergence from natural evolutionary forces. As far as we know, the total personality is a function of the biological organism transacting in a social and cultural context. There is no credible evidence that life survives the death of the body. We continue to exist in our progeny and in the way that our lives have influenced others in our culture.

According to the humanists, the universe is not created. Mankind evolved by natural processes. What is important is this life only—there is no afterlife. Instead of prayer, one should cultivate a feeling of well-being. Celebrating God and Jesus has no place in the modern world and is actually harmful to human life. We must make up our own morality and save ourselves. We should try to live together in harmony.

The *Manifestos* were drafted and signed by prominent members of the intellectual elite in the western world. There were two groups who found common ground, the so-called religious humanists and the secular humanists. Religious humanists wanted to reshape religion within a naturalistic framework, while the secularists were not interested in religion as such. Together they attempted to put brakes on the humanist vehicle—the perceived slippery slope of their own philosophy that led to the kind of atrocities that were manifested in the twentieth century. More people died in the twentieth century in the name of atheism than died in the name of religion in all recorded human history. The humanists of the *Manifesto* were concerned to preserve the optimistic view of human nature in the face of the terrible fruit of their philosophy as practiced by like-minded individuals who wielded political power.

Herbert Schlossberg, in his category "Idols of Humanity," argues that laws are always theologically based.[1] In the case of a humanist system, man takes the place of God. Since this is so, no action can be judged as absolutely good or evil. Schlossberg argues that with the increase of equality, the poorer classes have become ever more dissatisfied. This is opposite to what the humanists had expected, but is understandable if they serve idols of wealth that can never satisfy the human heart. He argues that humanism begins by lifting man up to godhood—but ends by pouring contempt on mankind. Thus the greatest humanists committed the worst crimes in the twentieth century, such as the purges of Stalin and Mao.

Francis Schaeffer and C. Everett Koop dedicate their joint effort "to those who were robbed of life, the unborn, the weak, the sick, the old, during the dark days of madness, selfishness, lust and greed for which the last decades of the twentieth century are remembered."[2] They argue that when the culture is informed by Christian values, people are valued as made in God's image. Once the belief in mankind's special nature is lost, however, no philosophical basis remains for treating people well. Humanists then necessarily move toward abusing genetic knowledge, since this is where they hope to escape the bondage of nature. As this philosophy permeates society, many societal ills increase rather than decrease, such as child abuse, abortion, and infanticide. Hitler was able to justify murdering millions who did not measure up to his arbitrary standard of what qualifies as fully human. Today, the unborn are similarly not protected and considered subhuman under the law. The *Humanist Manifestos* were written in part to speak against abusing people in the name of humanism, yet it is their very system that actually justifies this abuse. They are arguing not only against Christianity, but also against humanists wielding power.

Daniel 6 puts forward an image of man being worshipped to the exclusion of any deity. The world gives no resistance to this at all and complies, except for Daniel, who has the benefit of knowing the true and living God. Man and his works are worshipped by the culture. To reverence only God invites persecution. To follow the culture is to become an unthinking robotic sheep that can never be fulfilled. To keep one's eyes on the living God will enable one to avoid this temptation.

Jesus told the Jews to give to Caesar what is Caesar's and to God what is God's (Matt. 22:21). By defying the immutable law of the Medes and Persians, Daniel practiced what believers throughout the ages must practice when confronted with governments hostile to the commands of God. When the authorities told Peter and John to cease preaching the gospel, they replied, "We cannot help speaking about what we have seen and heard" (Acts 4:18–21). In 1 Peter 4:12–19, Christians are told not to be surprised when the inevitable ordeal of persecution comes, as long as they suffer for Christ and for what is right, and not for evil-doing. It is normal to suffer for Christ, not something strange or unexpected. Daniel, then, serves as an excellent model for all believers, and the obvious lesson is to "go and do likewise." Many in our own culture are persuaded by the humanists, and when and where they gain political power Christians are treated as the enemy. We need to remember Daniel and the lions' den, and render to God what is God's, despite the decrees of Caesar.

THE LIONS' DEN

Just as the reader discovers with Nebuchadnezzar what transpired in the fiery furnace, so does one discover with Darius the fate of Daniel in the lions' den. Both powerful monarchs learn and change and grow. "A close reading of characterization and point of view in Daniel 1–6 reveals . . . that the principal characters in the Daniel stories (with the exception of Daniel 1) are not the Judean sages, but the foreign sovereigns."[3] The surprising discoveries made by both kings, and their responses of faith, constitute the climax of both stories. This God was unfathomable to them, although intimately known to the persecuted Jews. The despots were surprised by the unexpected outcomes; the reader is meant to feel their astonishment.

Daniel was cast into the den of lions. A stone was rolled in front of the opening and it was sealed with wax. It is as if Daniel were sealed into a tomb. The description of the burial of Jesus is written in a manner that sounds like Daniel's "burial." Daniel was not just almost dead; he was within the sphere of death, abandoned to consumption. To emerge from there unscathed is to be brought back from annihilation.

The great reversal of this chapter, of course, is the discovery the next morning that Daniel was unhurt. Not a bone of his was broken, in contrast to what happens next to his accusers (6:24). Daniel cried out from the pit, "O king, live for ever! My God sent his angel and shut the lions' mouths, and they have not hurt me, because I was found blameless before him; and also before you, O king, I have done no wrong" (Dan. 6:21–22 RSV). God vindicated an innocent sufferer who was abandoned to the grave.

Matthew's account of Jesus' burial reads somewhat like the account of Daniel's being sealed in the pit; Daniel's emergence unhurt parallels Jesus' resurrection. Not a bone of his was broken, which is an important observation in John 19:36, highlighting Jesus as the Passover lamb, the bones of which should not be broken (Exod. 12:46). Also, Daniel is introduced in Daniel 1:4 as having no "blemish"— a word with cultic significance in Leviticus 21–24 (e.g., Lev. 22:20, "You shall not offer anything that has a blemish" [RSV]). Here, near the end of the first half of Daniel, the stories conclude with a cultic reference, Daniel once again being associated with a sacrificial offering.

Thus, we have a faithful Jew returning from a death inflicted by wild beasts, as an example for every saint. But the picture is bigger than that. Daniel's fate echoes the fate of all the Jews: "Will evildoers never learn—those who devour my people as men eat bread and who do not call on the LORD?" (Ps. 14:4); "They are like a lion hungry for prey, like a great lion crouching in cover" (Ps. 17:12); "A lion has come out of his lair; a destroyer of nations has set out. He has left his place to lay waste your land. Your towns will lie in ruins without inhabitant" (Jer. 4:7). The curse of wild beasts is the penalty for covenant infidelity (Deut. 32:24). What Daniel experienced is the common experience of all Israel, which has been devoured by Babylon and swallowed up. With the restoration of Daniel, however, one sees a glimmer of hope that perhaps all Israel also will experience restoration. One man, devoured by the pit, and then returning from there, personifies all the saints—given over to death by fearsome forces, then against all hope being restored and seeing their enemies vanquished instead. One man is needed, who is in reality what Daniel is only in symbol. We need one morally perfect, blemish-free man who really does die on behalf of his people, who really is brought back from Sheol, and in so doing destroys the real enemy—the pit itself. Amen, come, Lord Jesus!

The jealous courtiers "ate the pieces of the Jews" (Dan. 3:8). Nebuchadnezzar "ate grass like cattle" (4:33). Daniel's accusers "ate his pieces" (6:24). In chapter 7, four beasts tear and rend each other and the saints. The nations are beast-like and seek to devour and consume the Jews. With Daniel in the lions' den, this motif takes on an immediate and concrete character—real lions really surround a saint! After this story, the nations are portrayed in dreams as beasts hungry to devour each other. Idolaters look at Babylon and see a great and beautiful, magnificent city. The saints see a ravenous beast. Revelation also portrays Babylon as a harlot drunk on the blood of the saints and riding a seven-headed beast on many waters which represent all peoples and nations and kingdoms (Rev. 17). The saints will be persecuted, but will be vindicated, and in the meantime they use the opportunity to glorify God (as in chap. 1).

This closes the half of Daniel that features stories, and sets the stage for the dreams and visions to follow, particularly of the son of man who stands over against bestial earthly kingdoms.

FOR FURTHER REFLECTION

1. Have you counted the cost of your discipleship? What has your witness to Jesus cost you?
2. When should a Christian disobey the government?
3. What aspects of your culture are shaped by humanism? How do you as a Christian respond to this?
4. Who is free, and who is trapped? Why is this so?
5. Daniel was brought up from the pit alive. How is this story cut from the same cloth as the gospel? What hope for Christians is found there?

IO

THE CLOUD RIDER

Daniel 7 begins the second half of the book, which is characterized by dreams and visions. It obviously belongs with chapter 8, another vision of great beasts. However, it is written in Aramaic. As such, it also belongs with the Aramaic, not the Hebrew, portion of Daniel. It is parallel to chapter 2, which opens the Aramaic section. There, Nebuchadnezzar dreams of a fourfold statue smashed by a great Rock which grows and fills the world. In chapter 7, Daniel dreams of four great beasts that vie for power, only to be replaced by one like a son of man, the saints, the kingdom of God. Although events in Daniel had progressed to the era of Cyrus, chapter 7 is a flashback to Belshazzar's reign, the period of the golden head of Nebuchadnezzar's dream. Thus chapters 2 and 7 have the same setting, another parallel. Chapter 7 serves to link together the two halves of the book. By genre it belongs with the visions of the second half, but it is an integral part of the Aramaic collection, balancing the chiasm. The book of Daniel is therefore a unity, and the second half cannot be separated from the first. (The Aramaic portion begins midway through 2:4, linking the first and second chapters.)

Chapter 7 is the center of Daniel, the crux of the two halves, and it also has a center: "These four great beasts are four kings who shall arise out of the earth. But the saints of the Most High shall receive the kingdom, and possess the kingdom for ever, for ever and ever" (7:17–18 RSV). Empires and nations of this world will pass away, and the saints will then receive the kingdom forever. This is a good summation of both halves of the book of Daniel.

In Daniel's night vision, four beasts rose from the sea. Here we find the demonology of the book of Daniel, the beasts arising from the dark underworld of malevolent spirits. The fourth beast was powerful and terrible, with horns and teeth of iron. It had a little horn with human eyes and a mouth that spoke boastful words. As Daniel watched, the glorious Ancient of Days took his judgment seat, and the last beast perished in the fire of judgment. One like a son of man came with the clouds of heaven and received glory and dominion and kingdom for ever and ever.

The second half of the chapter is a progressively more detailed interpretation of the vision. The four beasts are four kingdoms. The fourth is unlike the others, ravenous and terrible, and its little horn is an individual king who oppresses the saints and tries to change what God has decreed for them. But the divine court will judge him. The saints then inherit an everlasting kingdom.

BEASTS AND HORNS

The *pesher* in 7:16–18 gives a thumbnail sketch of the meaning of the vision. The four beasts are four kingdoms that will dominate until the saints begin their rule. The earthly kingdoms will come to an end at the time that the eternal kingdom of the Most High is inaugurated. However, the *pesher* does not identify the kingdoms. As in chapter 2, there are three ways to read it—Babylon, Media, Persia, and Greece; Babylon, Medo-Persia, Greece, and Rome; or "four kingdoms symbolically representing the fact that evil kingdoms . . . will succeed one another . . . to the time of the climax of history."[1] If the second beast (like a bear) is Medo-Persia, any bifurcation in its description could be explained. If the third or fourth animal is Greece, any split into two or four could be explained. (Daniel 11 is about the Greek world divided in two; historically it had also split into four parts.)

The first beast was a cherub, a lion with eagle's wings. The avian features were ripped away, and it was made to stand like a man, experiencing an inner change—"the heart of a man was given to it" (7:4). This is reminiscent of chapter 4, where Nebuchadnezzar was given "the mind of an animal" (4:16). His hair "had grown like eagles" (4:33). The Aramaic text says "eagles," which in English is glossed "eagle's feathers." Jeremiah 4:7 refers to Nebuchadnezzar as a lion, and Ezekiel 17:3–4, 11–12 refers to him as an eagle. The first beast, in the end, became more human and less bestial. The beast was not autonomous, but utterly subordinate to whatever power could transform it. God is absolutely sovereign over kings and kingdoms. The saints can be assured of this and take heart.

The second beast is like a bear with one side raised and preeminent. This is a bifurcated feature, perhaps hinting that the creature is complex, an image for both Media and Persia, with Persia possessing the superior status. Historically, Persia gradually gained dominance over Media. Or perhaps the creature is reared up on its hind legs and made to stand like a man, exhibiting human characteristics like the cherub. It is crunching on three unidentified ribs. Jeremiah 51:27–28 lists three allies of Media; or perhaps they are simply the cherub's remains? Again, the carnivore is not autonomous, being told, "Get up and eat your fill of flesh!" It does not act on its own, but only does as instructed and permitted.

The third beast was like a leopard with four bird's wings and four heads, a fourfold kingdom. Historically, Alexander's kingdom broke up into four parts, two of which contended over Palestine. Persia did not break up into four kingdoms; neither did it conquer the Medes. The beast's wings and cat-like velocity (like a cheetah's) highlight its blazing speed. The goat of Daniel 8:5 ran so fast its feet never touched the ground (also seeming to fly). Alexander conquered the known world in just a few years. The goat is called Greece, which charges a ram that is called Medo-Persia (8:20–21). This feline's fourfold makeup might indicate Alexander's Greek empire. On the other hand, "four" symbolically represents universality, as in the "four winds" of Daniel 7:2. There are also four beasts, indicating that the vision speaks of the universality of human kingdoms. Again, the cat "was given authority to rule"—another reminder of the complete sovereignty of God over it.

The fourth beast is a monstrosity, partly of iron and bronze. It tramples everything. Its ten horns recall the semi-ferrous ten toes of Nebuchadnezzar's dream-statue. Its ten horns are ten kings (7:24). This beast represents either Greece or Rome. It is the culmination of earthly powers rivaling God and intolerant of his saints. A little horn with human features rooted up three other horns, saying pompous things. Nothing is said in the *pesher* of the sovereign will of God and this horn—it simply boasts after uprooting about one-third of the others. Note that in Revelation the horns or trumpets ruin one-third of the earth.

The horn is the power of an animal; a bull is alarming when its head is down and it charges with horns pointed at you! Symbolically, a horn is a nation's power (Ps. 89:17, 24; Jer. 48:25). It also is a symbol of an individual's glory and strength—either for or against God (1 Sam. 2:1; Ps. 75:5). God's strength is his horn, which he lifts up against his enemies to save his people (Ps. 112:9; 2 Sam. 22:3; Luke 1:67–69). The little horn is a king who will rule a kingdom after the ten horns. He will oppress the saints and try to change the law, creating new morality and new religious festivals (7:24–25), for a time, times, and half a time. If the fourth kingdom is Greece, then the little horn comes from or after the Greek kingdom; if Rome, the little horn comes from or after Rome. Perhaps he is a late-coming conqueror, arising long after the monstrous kingdom.

After depicting the arrogant boasting of earthly kingdoms, the scene abruptly changes to a vision of heaven. One from antiquity, of great age, with shining white clothing and face, sits on his war-chariot to judge. A river of fire flows from this chariot to consume his enemies. An uncountable host serves him. The books are opened, and judgment is rendered. The Heavenly Court stands over all earthly kingdoms and hands over authority to the saints. There is no battle in the end. The Ancient of Days simply declares his verdict based on law, and the sentence is carried out. No appeal is tried, and the horn's boastful words are exposed as so much empty talk. This is the climax of human history.

Today, Christians live in an age filled with boastful words against the Most High God. Darius was to be worshipped to the exclusion of any god. But Christians can take heart that the world's arrogance will suddenly pop like a bubble, exposed as hollow and empty. The meek will inherit the earth. History is inexorably moving towards the climax when the saints are vindicated and revealed as those who were right, in the end justified for their clinging to the name of Jesus.

ONE LIKE A SON OF MAN

Before the Ancient of Days stands one like a son of man over against the four beasts and their horns (7:11–14). He is the opposite of them, the antidote to them. He comes victoriously, riding with the clouds. The Ancient of Days sits in a wheeled throne—a fiery chariot. Both divine persons are fit for war, willing and able to judge and vanquish their enemies. Consider the violence of the conflict in Daniel. The kingdom of God smashed the world-kingdoms to bits (2:44). Fire broke out and consumed the guards who were following orders (3:22), and the king threatened to tear limb from limb any who spoke against God (3:29). The enemies of God were shattered by wild beasts (6:24). The fourth beast shall trample and crush the whole earth (7:23). On and on violence is done by nations, kings, peoples, and thus they provoke God (and contrite kings!) to vengeance. God is always at war with those who afflict the saints. "If anyone destroys God's temple, God will destroy him; for God's temple is sacred, and you are that temple" (1 Cor. 3:17). Daniel 7 is a glimpse into the character of God the divine warrior, who brings history to its inevitable conclusion with the final defeat of all his enemies. The divine cloud rider comes in glory—and judgment is rendered.[2] The son of man—the cloud rider—who comes to conquer, is echoed in chapter 10 by Michael, the warrior of heaven who fights for the saints.

The Ancient of Days has hair *like* wool, garments white *like* snow. The beasts are not described as being a "lion," "bear," or "leopard." Rather, they are *like* these creatures; bear-like, lion-like, and so forth. In the same way, set off against the beasts is one *like* a "son of man"—that is, one who is *human*, not bestial. The beasts are symbols of nations, kingdoms, corporate groups of peoples. In the context of this vision, the son of man also represents a corporate entity that embodies human, not bestial qualities. The *raz*, the mystery, is the identity of the son of man; the *pesher* is that he symbolizes the saints. The *pesher* is revealed to Daniel: "The four great beasts are four kingdoms that will rise from the earth. But the saints of the Most High will receive the kingdom and will possess it forever" (Dan.

7:17–18). Once the son of man is seen in all his glory, the chapter does not mention him again, but instead speaks of the saints. The son of man symbolizes the saints in contrast to the demonic nation-beasts.

But who are the saints? The Hebrew word *qaddish* can be glossed "saints," "sanctified," "holy," "sacred." "Kadesh" is the name of a city (Num. 33:37). The "saints" or "holy ones" occur a number of times in Daniel 7. They are *qaddishe 'elyonin*, "holy ones of the Most High" (7:18), who take possession of the kingdom (7:22) and will be worn out by the little horn (7:25). The little horn prevails over the holy ones (7:21). Daniel 7:27 has the phrase *'am qaddishe 'elyonin*, "people of the holy ones of the Most High," elsewhere *'am qedoshim*, "people of the holy ones" (8:24), and "watchers and holy ones from heaven" (4:17, 23); in Daniel 4:17 the holy ones command and the watchers decree (see also Dan. 8:13–16). Elsewhere in Scripture, the Holy One is God, and "holy ones" are angels, such as in Deuteronomy 33:2. Sometimes holy ones are faithful Israelites (Ps. 79:2; 85:8; 116:15).

There are two views regarding their identity in Daniel 7; the saints are either angels or Israelites.[3] In the Old Testament, "holy ones" usually refers to angels. In Daniel 7:13 the son of man is a divine figure coming with heavenly clouds; since the holy ones are identified with him (7:18), they must also be divine. "Like" a son of man means that he *isn't* a son of man. The holy ones are the host of heaven, whose human counterparts are "the saints, the people of the Most High" (7:27). The vision is of a heavenly assault on earthly kingdoms that shake their fists against heaven and oppress the people of the heavenly host.

On the other hand, Israel elsewhere in the Old Testament is promised a kingdom with an anointed king; no such promise is made to angels. The saints receive a kingdom over against earthly powers, and terrestrial kings cannot oppress angels (7:21–25)! The phrase "people of the holy ones" should be read "people who are saints"; it is hardly speaking of angels—the holy ones are people, people oppressed.

Both views have merit. But Jesus spoke of the Son of Man coming with the clouds, gathering up his elect from the four winds. Here is a *pesher* to the Son of Man as a divine figure, with the elect—the saints—identified with him and ushered by him into heaven, in effect becoming angels (Matt. 24:30–31). The moral of the story is to stay alert, because the Son of Man will come when not expected (Matt. 24:42–44). The chief priest demanded to know if Jesus was the Messiah, the Son of God, and Jesus answered, "Yes, it is as you say. . . . But I say to all of you: In the future you will see the Son of Man sitting at the right hand of the Mighty One and coming on the clouds of heaven" (Matt. 26:59–64). In Daniel, the divine son of man represents oppressed saints, probably faithful Israelites, who inherit the kingdom—but the term *qaddish* usually refers to celestial beings. Jesus sees himself as the Son of Man, and envisions the elect translated into heaven with angels at his coming. Can the son of man in Daniel be one person and at the same time a figure that symbolizes the saints?

The great forces in history are treated in Daniel symbolically as corporate entities. The beasts of the visions represent people-groups and societies as a unit, with one or two defining characteristics. However, in chapter 2, the golden head stood for the nation of Babylon *and* for Nebuchadnezzar individually. In a sense, Nebuchadnezzar is Babylon (2:38–39). In chapter 7, the saints have their lot in common. Together they are handed over and oppressed (7:25), and together they possess the kingdom (7:22). Jehoiakim is given to Nebuchadnezzar, and with him, all Israel (1:2). In chapter 9, Daniel pleads before God on behalf of his people in sackcloth and ashes, although he as an individual enjoys wealth and power in Babylon. Daniel's identity is bound up with his people and his God. Individuals derive their self-identity with respect to their people, and the people's king shares the fate of the kingdom.

"Speaking the truth in love, we will in all things grow up into him who is the Head, that is, Christ. From him the whole body, joined and held together by every supporting ligament, grows and builds itself up in love, as each part does its work" (Eph. 4:15–16). Jesus is the head of the church. He is an individual, yet he also represents and embodies his people. He died in place of his people. Christians share in his resurrection. "And he is the head of the body, the church; he is the beginning and the firstborn from among the dead, so that in everything he might have the supremacy" (Col. 1:18). "You are those who have stood by me in my trials. And I confer on you a kingdom, just as my Father conferred one on me, so that you may eat and drink at my table in my kingdom and sit on thrones, judging the twelve tribes of Israel" (Luke 22:28–30). "Here is a trustworthy saying: If we died with him, we will also live with him; if we endure, we will also reign with him" (2 Tim. 2:11–12).

Christ is the head of the church, and the church consists in him. Adam sinned and so the whole human race is guilty before God. David stood as champion—as it went with David against Goliath so it would go with Israel. Christ stood for his people, and they inherit a kingdom with him; he is the One who stands for and represents the church. Similarly, the vision of the son of man who inherits the kingdom is more than a symbol that represents the saints. He is the champion of the saints; when he inherits the kingdom, the saints do also with him. The son of man is king of the saints, just as the little horn is king of a people and Nebuchadnezzar is king of Babylon. As it goes with him, so it goes with his people. "Do you not know that the saints will judge the world?" (1 Cor. 6:2).

Another interesting aspect of Daniel's vision is that those who receive the kingdom, represented in the son of man, are called the saints of the Most High, 'elyonin. But the word 'elyonin, "Most High," is a plural word. Technically, the saints are the people of the Most High Ones. There are two divine figures in Daniel's vision: the Ancient of Days, and the one like a son of man who comes with the clouds. The saints are the people of the Father and the Son. "The Father judges no one, but has entrusted all judgment to the Son, that all may honor the Son just as they honor the Father. He who does not honor the Son does not honor the Father, who sent him" (John 5:22–23).

CHRIST AND THE SAINTS

The little horn wears out the saints, but is judged before the son of man and the Ancient of Days. This is perhaps the cardinal image in the book of Daniel—Jesus standing before the judgment seat of God, vindicating his people against their enemies.

In the vision, however, it is not the son of man who suffers—it is the saints. They are oppressed and worn down by their enemies, but the son of man does not do battle nor suffer. This seems contrary to the gospel, which teaches that the Son of Man will suffer for his people. Jesus said, "The Son of Man is going to be betrayed into the hands of men. They will kill him, and after three days he will rise" (Mark 9:31). Jane Schaberg finds three parallels when she compares this to Daniel 7:25: "And they [the saints] shall be given into his [the little horn's] hand for a time, two times, and half a time" (RSV).[4] First, in the old Greek translation, the verb "shall be given," paradidōmi, is used in Mark to describe handing over the Son of Man. Second, the phrase "into the hands of" is used in both accounts. Finally, the vindication of the Son of Man, says Jesus, will occur "after three days," while the saints in Daniel suffer for a time, times, and half a time. Figure 6 illustrates these parallels.

Figure 6
Parallels between Daniel 7:25–27 and Mark 9:31

Daniel 7:25–27	Mark 9:31
The saints	The Son of Man
will be delivered to (*paradidōmi*)	
a blasphemous king (little horn)	evil men.
for a time, times, half time.	After three days
The court will sit, the power of the horn will be destroyed forever, and the kingdom will be handed to the saints.	he will rise.

Daniel 12:1–2 reveals that the resurrection of the saints is what Daniel ultimately has in view:

> At that time Michael, the great prince who protects your people, will arise. There will be a time of distress such as has not happened from the beginning of nations until then. But at that time your people—everyone whose name is found written in the book—will be delivered. Multitudes who sleep in the dust of the earth will awake: some to everlasting life, others to shame and everlasting contempt.

So if the son of man shares in the sufferings of the saints (taking the interpretive lead from Jesus), he also shares in their vindication—by rising from the dead. As it is with the saints (7:25, sufferings; 12:2, resurrection), so it is with the son of man.

After his resurrection, Jesus opened the Scriptures to his disciples. He explained to them all the things in the Old Testament concerning himself and his gospel.

Then he said to them, "These are my words which I spoke to you, while I was still with you, that everything written about me in the law of Moses and the prophets and the psalms must be fulfilled." Then he opened their minds to understand the scriptures, and said to them, "Thus it is written, that the Christ should suffer and on the third day rise from the dead, and that repentance and forgiveness of sins should be preached in his name to all nations, beginning from Jerusalem." (Luke 24:44–47 RSV)

Perhaps it was from Daniel's vision that Jesus taught that the Christ must suffer, and a time, times, and half a time later rise from the dead. The gospel then would be preached in his name to all nations.

In Daniel's vision, the saints are not identified by nationality. They are not explicitly called Israelites. As argued before, apocalyptic has some connections with wisdom literature, where redemptive themes that run throughout the Bible seem to recede into the background. One of those themes is the identity of Israel as a special people of God. In Daniel 7, the saints are not explicitly identified, but their kingdom replaces the kingdoms of the world. The great people-groups continue on after the destruction of the fourth beast (Dan. 7:12). The book of Revelation was written long after Alexander's kingdom had passed on and Rome became dominant. John wrote (Rev. 13) of a beast rising from the sea, with ten horns, energized by Satan. This beast uttered blasphemous words and persecuted the saints, now understood as a people taken from every nation and kingdom. This viewpoint stretches beyond Rome throughout world history to the final end of time (as Daniel's vision does). Throughout history, Christians are persecuted by world powers that seek to rival God. While we wait for the court to sit in judgment and the coming of the Son of Man, we are called to be wise (Rev. 17:9). Daniel's reaction to his dream (7:28) was to be deeply troubled. His face turned pale. He was appalled and confused. Christians would do well to steel themselves for the coming persecution, all the more as we see the Day approaching.

FOR FURTHER REFLECTION

1. How ready are you for persecution? Do you assume trouble won't come? Why or why not?
2. Is a Christian who is overwhelmed for an extended period of time with a strong emotion failing to trust God? List believers in the Bible who struggled with feelings of grief, depression, or anxiety.
3. Consider how comforting it is to know that your faith will be vindicated in the end.
4. In the New Testament, who is the Son of Man? What does Daniel teach about him? What path to greatness did he choose, as opposed to the beasts with their horns?

PART THREE

THE HEBREW PORTION:
THE BRONZE AGE

The book of Daniel reverts back to Hebrew for the next section. The traditional reading of Daniel identifies this with the bronze era of Nebuchadnezzar's dream-statue. From the perspective of the Aramaic portion, this material is future. As the great powers in the past subjected the Jews, casting them into the flames and giving them over to wild beasts, so kings will arise in future kingdoms to do the same, until the end.

This history begins with the penultimate little horn, the king who serves in history as a type of the last evil king to come. The veil is pulled back to reveal warring spiritual forces in the heavenly realms before the final revelation of history begins, delineating endless wars on earth that buffet and wear out the saints.

11

THE PENULTIMATE
LITTLE HORN

Daniel 8 begins the Hebrew portion, the second large block of material in Daniel. Chapters 8–11 describe the heinous evil the saints will face in near history as a precursor to the apocalyptic end of time. What transpires in the centuries after Daniel has some similarities to the state of affairs in eschatological time, when the saints will be Christians of every people-group, and the persecuting powers unimaginatively greater than those faced by faithful Jews under foreign domination in the postexilic crises. The periods of Medo-Persia and the Greeks are detailed in chapters 8–11 of Daniel, and are meant to be read as a paradigm of all of history, culminating in a final conflict, a universal resurrection, and the inauguration of the rule of the saints.

TWO GREAT BEASTS

The vision takes place again in the period of the golden head of Nebuchadnezzar's dream, the Babylonian era.

Daniel saw a ram with two horns of different height charging and glorifying itself, and none could withstand it. Its "butting" behavior, as it does whatever it pleases, is echoed in Daniel 11:36, 40, describing the king of the South. (There are other parallels, such as "furiously" in 8:7 and "in a rage" in 11:11, and "four winds of heaven" in 8:8 and 11:4. This highlights the connection between these chapters.) In the *pesher*, the ram symbolizes Medo-Persia, with each horn representing a people-group, Persia catching up with and eventually surpassing Media.

Daniel then saw a swift goat with a single prominent horn, its feet not touching the ground. The goat destroyed the ram. At the height of its glory, the goat's horn was broken off, to be replaced by four others. According to the *pesher*, this goat is Greece, and the first king will be replaced with four others, who each will rule over a piece of the original kingdom. Out of one of those four kingdoms, Daniel saw a little horn. It grew great, even to the point of casting down the stars of heaven. This is the *pesher*:

> A king of bold countenance, one who understands riddles, shall arise. His power shall be great, and he shall cause fearful destruction, and shall succeed in what he does, and destroy mighty men and the people of the saints. By his cunning he shall make deceit prosper under his hand, and in his own mind he shall magnify himself. Without warning he shall destroy many; and he shall even rise up against the Prince of princes; but, by no human hand, he shall be broken. (Dan. 8:23–25 RSV)

In chapter 8, Daniel sees two great beasts; in chapter 7, four. How do these visions coincide? If the four brutes of chapter 7 are Babylon, Media, Persia, and Greece, then the ram is both the bear and the leopard, and the goat is the monster. If the four animals are Babylon, Medo-Persia,

Greece, and Rome, then the ram is the bear and the goat is the leopard. By analyzing the features of the goat and comparing it to chapter 7, chapter 8 can be used to help determine whether the leopard or the monster is Greece. This is graphically represented in figure 7.

Figure 7
Interpretive Schemes of the Beasts of Daniel 7 and 8

Chapter 8		Chapter 7		Chapter 8
	Babylon	Lion	*Babylon*	
Ram {	*Media*	Bear	*Medo-Persia*	Ram
	Persia	Leopard	*Greece*	Goat
Goat	*Greece*	Monster	*Rome*	

The goat had a prominent horn (Alexander the Great). It ran so swiftly it seemed to fly. It shattered Medo-Persia, which is conceptualized as a unit. Four horns took the place of the single horn "toward the four winds of heaven," thus introducing a fourfold quality to the goat. Out of one of the four horns came a little horn that started small but grew great in the south and east. It threw some of the starry host down, rivaled the Prince of the host, and desolated the sanctuary.

The leopard had four wings and four heads. It destroyed the bear, and was the second-to-last kingdom before the end. The monster was terrifying, with iron teeth, and trampled the leopard. It is the last beast mentioned. It had ten horns, and a little horn.

Chapter 7 is written in Aramaic, and chapter 8 in Hebrew. Even so, the description of the monster—that it was terrifying, powerful, and trampled its victims—seems purposely to avoid cognates with the goat. The expected verbal correspondences are absent—strange if they shared a common referent (Greece).[1] The leopard shares its fourfold quality with the goat. Nothing significant connects the monster and the goat except the little horn. If the little horn of the monster is the little horn of the goat, then the monster and the goat (and the iron era of chapter 2) are Greece. To determine the identity of the monster, the two little horns can be compared.

THE LITTLE HORN IN HISTORY

The monster's little horn of chapter 7 uprooted three other horns. It spoke boastfully and acted big (although it never actually grew big). It waged war with the saints and tried to change the sacred calendar and laws for a time, times, and half a time. It was finally destroyed in spectacular fashion with the monster when the court was held, and the saints who had been persecuted then inherited the kingdom. The goat's little horn of chapter 8 started small but grew in power toward the Beautiful Land. Its insignificant origin and growth in size are highlighted. It threw down stars and trampled them. Perhaps this indicates claims to divinity, or perhaps the stars represent earthly kings. It compared itself to the "Prince of the host" (God). It took away daily sacrifices, and desolated the sanctuary for not quite a time, times, and half a time (3 1/2 years), that is, for something like 3 years and 2 1/2 months. Finally, the horn was broken off, and history continued on, with no reward for saints as yet.

The two little horns are different enough that a sensitive reader must conclude that they are no more representative of the same person than any other horns in the visions of Daniel. The little horn of chapter 7 is judged at the end of time; in chapter 8 the little horn is just one particularly nasty king in history, but history continues on after his fall. The leopard, then, is clearly Greece, and the monster is clearly a kingdom that arose after Greece, namely Rome (although its little horn arose much later). Thus Daniel sees history moving forward up to and including the empire that ruled when Christ came and was subjected to death for a time, times, and half a time.

The large original horn on the goat was Alexander the Great, who very quickly conquered the known world. He suddenly died at age thirty-three, leaving no heirs. His kingdom was divided by four generals, who are the four prominent horns. Ptolemy ruled Egypt; Seleucus, Syria; Lysimachus ruled Thrace; Cassander, Macedonia and Greece. The Egyptian and Syrian kingdoms overlapped at Palestine, and, accordingly, in the years to come Palestine became the battleground between these two states, Egypt to the south and Syria to the north.

The vision then speaks of a little horn that came up out of one of the four horns. This is Antiochus IV Epiphanes, who became king of Syria about two hundred years later. The skipped two hundred years are covered in some detail in chapter 11 of Daniel. (Just as chapter 8's little horn arises centuries after the goat-kingdom fractures, so chapter 7's little horn will arise long after Rome loses superpower status.)

Antiochus championed Greek (Hellenistic) culture throughout his kingdom. He wanted to make Jerusalem a Greek city. So he banned the Sabbath observance, circumcision, and the study of Torah. He erected an altar to the Greek gods and forced Jews to make sacrifice. On pain of death he forced them to eat pork. He stole the furnishings of the temple. He pressured the Jews to yield their faith.

Some Jews went along with the times and made themselves into Gentiles by surgically removing the marks of circumcision. They built a gymnasium in Jerusalem. Antiochus corrupted the priesthood by appointing an illegitimate priest; he called the temple the temple of Zeus. However, most of the population rejected Hellenistic culture and were true to their religion and traditions.

Finally, in 167 B.C., Jews began to revolt against this domination. They could see that the end of their culture was at stake. After a long and difficult struggle, they cleansed the temple and repealed Antiochus's decrees, making Judea (briefly) an independent state. Antiochus died, and the Roman Empire began to extend its rule into the Beautiful Land. The little horn was finally broken off. It was not followed, however, by the saints inheriting the kingdom but, rather, by the rise of a monstrous and powerful state that would kill the Lord of glory on a cross.

THE *PESHER* AND THE *RAZ*

Once given the *pesher* and being told that the vision is about Greece defeating Medo-Persia, can the reader then dispense with the cryptic symbols of ram and goat? If Gabriel's message completely exegetes the *raz*, and if the goal of interpretation is to decode the mystery, why then is the mystery preserved? What is gained by reading about two brutes that is not better gained by reading about what they mean? The tedious material above illustrates how hard it is to decide what represents what. Daniel does not speak plainly and will not clearly state what he means! But once the reader understands what each beast represents, why retain the vision? Can the *raz* be reduced to the *pesher*?

There is more to the symbol than a mere equation of goat = Greece. The goat has personality, a life of its own. The symbols substitute for "facts," but are bigger and richer than facts. "One like a son of man," who stands before the Ancient of Days (7:13), as well as the chief prince Michael waging cosmic battle for the saints (10:13), give the reader a glimpse behind the scenes in a reality that transcends the believer's miserable existence. These pictures help the reader conceptualize a God-centered world. The symbols are larger than life. They stick in the mind and convey far more meaning than simply one military campaign after another. What does the *raz* reveal that the *pesher* does not? Nothing less than the savage, insane terror of future regimes. The reader is supposed to equate Alexander's empire with a ravaging brute. This helps keep a sane head when proud empires claim to rival God.

Sometimes people who are suffering are unable to grasp a systematic, logical argument. Children learn best with illustrations and pictures. Getting the point across through imagery is sometimes the best vehicle of communication. Daniel models the language of picture. A reader may forget the details of the *pesher*; Alexander and Antiochus may be unknown. But a succession of terrible beasts that devoured one another and trampled the saints, under the leadership of a blasphemous horn with eyes and a mouth? Everyone will remember *that*.

When Antiochus IV Epiphanes died, the kingdom was not ushered in, in any sense. Chapter 8 affirms this. But the little horn of chapter 7 is referring to some world power that persecutes the saints until they receive the kingdom. Thus, there are two little horns—the ultimate horn at the denouement of history (chap. 7), and the penultimate horn similar to it, Antiochus Epiphanes (chap. 8). Antiochus is like a future king or nation or government yet to arise, the culmination of the anti-God impulse of those who persecute the saints. To look at what Antiochus did to the Jews is to see in advance what the final blasphemous king will do to Christians.

Christ ushered in a new age. His resurrection is the first fruit of those who will rise at the end of time—and thus the resurrection at the end of the world has started. The baptism of fire that will engulf the world is now poured out on Christians, as they are immersed in the Holy Spirit and suffer for the sake of Christ. Salvation is accomplished, it is finished; the end of the world is begun in Christ. A penultimate little horn arose somewhat before the beginning of the end of the world. His name was Antiochus. In the same way, an ultimate little horn will arise before the end of the end of the world, a king yet to be seen.

Figure 8 is borrowed from Richard Patterson.[2] Notice the little horns: the little horn of chapter 8 is set parallel to the king of the North of chapters 10–12. The little horn of chapter 7 is set parallel to the willful king of chapter 11. In fact, there may be many penultimate little horns that arise before the ultimate.

Figure 8
The Kingdoms and Symbols of Daniel

Chapter	2	7	8	9 (Keil)	10–12
Babylon	Golden head	Winged lion			
Medo-Persia	Silver chest	Bear on its side	Ram	Decree to rebuild;	Four kings
Greece	Bronze belly	Leopard with four wings and heads	Goat	7 sevens; Anointed One	Mighty king + successors
Antiochus			Little horn		Kings of the North
Rome	Iron legs, clay toes	Dreadful beast		62 sevens	
Last evil king		Little horn		1 seven	Willful king
Final kingdom	Rock	Son of man		The End	Resurrection, felicity

EMOTIONAL RESPONSE

Daniel was "appalled" (8:27)—the same Hebrew word as used for "desolate" in "abomination of desolation" (8:13). He was emotionally distressed enough to lie ill for days in bed, but not because he had a spiritual problem. He was overwhelmed with the horror of the years ahead that the saints would have to endure—this was a godly emotional depression.[3]

Christians sometimes treat prophecy as if it were something fun to study, an amusing diversion, a mentally stimulating exercise in puzzle-solving. But the visions of Daniel were emotionally traumatic to their recipients. There was a dark backdrop of loss and pain that was ever-present in the hearts and minds of the Jews in exile. "Why should not my face be sad, when the city, the place of my fathers' sepulchers, lies waste, and its gates have been destroyed by fire?" (Neh. 2:3 RSV). Daniel's visions were intended to inspire hope in the hearts of persecuted and suffering saints when the predicted terrible events happened. The saints were forewarned so they would not be surprised and doubt that God is in control.

Christians also know the future:

> For nation will rise against nation, and kingdom against kingdom, and there will be famines and earthquakes in various places: all this is but the beginning of the birth-pangs. Then they will deliver you up to tribulation, and put you to death; and you will be hated by all nations for my name's sake. And then many will fall away, and betray one another, and hate one another. And many false prophets will arise and lead many astray. And because wickedness is multiplied, most men's love will grow cold. But he who endures to the end will be saved. And this gospel of the kingdom will be preached throughout the whole world, as a testimony to all nations; and then the end will come. (Matt. 24:7–14 RSV)

He who endures to the end will be saved, and the gospel will first be preached throughout the world. Jesus then cites Daniel's vision of the desolation of abomination and instructs his disciples what to do when that happens again.

FOR FURTHER REFLECTION

1. How is theology implanted into the minds of sufferers?
2. How do you speak the truth to those in great pain?
3. Can you imagine a great civilization seen from the point of view of heaven as evil and beastlike due to its injustices and callous disregard of the saints of God? In what ways is your culture great; in what ways beastlike?
4. What can you do to ameliorate the suffering of the saints in this world?
5. As it goes with the saints, so it goes with the Son of Man. What does this imply about the career of the Son of Man?

12

SANITY

The prayer of Daniel (9:1–20) is a unique section. Elsewhere in Daniel, the book reads as sapiential material, similar to Proverbs or Ecclesiastes. But here characteristics appear that are otherwise absent. This is where God's covenantal name Yahweh is found (eight times in seven verses, as if making up for its absence elsewhere). In Daniel's prayer, the law of Moses is referred to by terms such as *mitsvah* ("commandment"), *mishpat* ("judgment"), and *torah* ("law") (9:4–5, 10). The Mosaic covenant is here uniquely at issue. The word *berit* ("covenant") occurs in 9:4 (and in 9:27, forming an inclusion which unites both halves of chapter 9). This Yahweh, who gave the law to Moses, is holding the Jews accountable to that law. This is why they are in exile. In such a situation, this Yahweh should be approached in petition with a humble heart. This is the only place in Daniel where the language of prayer, supplication, fasting, and sackcloth and ashes are found. This is the only place where the word "prophet" (*nabi'*) is used.

AN ANOMALOUS ELEMENT IN DANIEL

In chapter 1, the young Jews had no blemish. They were cultically pure and would not defile themselves with Babylonian *patbag*. They were heroes whose wisdom outshined the Chaldeans'. In chapter 3, the three Jews refused to bow to an idol, although the rest of the world did. They were thrown into the fiery furnace, yet in the end vindicated. The pagans were shown to be arrogant and sacrilegious; the Jews again are heroes of the faith. In chapter 4, Daniel begged Nebuchadnezzar to show mercy to the oppressed (4:27). God proved Daniel right, and the oppressor of the disadvantaged repented before God. In chapter 5, Belshazzar the evil king misused the vessels of Yahweh and was judged by God through the righteous Daniel. Through it all, Daniel was not culpable for any sin. In chapter 6, Daniel was again above reproach—the only accusation his enemies could make was about how devoted he was to God! Again, God vindicated Daniel and the pagans were condemned as evildoers. In chapter 7, the Israelites are called "saints" or "holy ones." They are not culpable for any misdeed, and are persecuted precisely because they hold fast to God in faith. In chapter 8, the little horn tramples the sanctuary and the saints suffer; the evil is not laid at their door, but entirely with the evil Antiochus. In chapters 10 and 11, the machinations and wars of godless kings are recounted, and in chapter 12 the wise will shine like stars. Throughout the book of Daniel, the Israelites are found faithful, and the pagans are organized into terrible, monstrous nations that tyrannize and persecute God's holy ones. The Jews are good, the pagans are bad.

However, this is all turned upside-down in Daniel's prayer. Daniel confesses that the Israelites have sinned against Yahweh, and so are justly being punished in exile. He sees that the nations are but tools in God's hands; it is not with them that the Jews have to do. The chapter begins with Daniel reading from the book of Jeremiah—imbibing redemptive history on the particularly Israelite understanding of the flow of events under the control of a righteous, sovereign God. In fact, Daniel borrows language from Jeremiah in his prayer. Daniel 9:17 uses a word glossed "desolate" and found elsewhere only in Jeremiah 12:11. Daniel seems to be reading through Jeremiah, thinking his thoughts after him, letting Jeremiah shape his thinking and his approach to God. Daniel recounts the history of Israel, citing Moses, the judges, the covenant, Jerusalem, and so on.

Unlike the rest of Daniel, this material is not wisdom literature. It is an almost entirely different way of approaching God than is found in the wisdom books. This has more affinity with Isaiah 58:5 or Nehemiah 9 and the dedication of the second temple, or 1 Kings 8 and the dedication of Solomon's temple. Here Daniel, with every Israelite, is in covenant with the God of his fathers. The tension between Daniel's prayer and the rest of the book is so smooth one might not notice it. Almost subliminally, the prayer connects Daniel with the rest of the Bible. It begins by linking with the prophecy of Jeremiah and the mystery of the seventy years. Daniel himself is living out the fulfillment of this prophecy. The perspective of Jeremiah is upheld for the reader, that God's law controls history for Israel.

Since Daniel's prayer associates the book with Jeremiah and the history of Israel, many terms in Daniel can be identified with certainty. The saints are those who trust in Yahweh throughout the unfolding of this history to its climactic end. The sanctuary is where Yahweh is worshipped. The times and laws that should not be changed are the order of worship God revealed at Sinai. The coming king, the son of man, is the one who rules the world for his people. It is no accident that immediately after connecting the book with prophecy (Jeremiah), a time frame is revealed in the rest of chapter 9 that culminates with putting an end to sin, atoning for iniquity, and bringing in everlasting righteousness (9:24).

The book of Daniel envisions a chain of apocalyptic events climaxing with the coming of Jesus to make atonement for sin, to fulfill prophecy, to die and after three days rise, then rule over the kingdom of the Most High for ever and ever. It is in Christ, and only in Christ, that Daniel is anything more than pie-in-the-sky wishful thinking. It is because the saints themselves need to be purified, atoned for, forgiven, and restored that Daniel prays as he does. Without this prayer, Daniel might be misunderstood as implying that the saints are perfect. His prayer highlights the dark background—that the saints are themselves a people under judgment who need atonement—which is elsewhere almost absent from the book. This is where Jesus is so necessary. He is the one who is truly a saint—perfectly pure, *really* without blemish, the Holy One of Israel, who can suffer for his people, making them saints, and so justifying their description in the rest of Daniel as saints who suffer unjustly.

DANIEL'S SANITY

Daniel 4 explores the insanity of hubris before the sovereign God. Nebuchadnezzar was the model of self-esteem, exulting in his own achievements. This was part and parcel of his insanity, however. The opposite of insanity was not his attitude before his affliction, but after.

At the end of that time, I, Nebuchadnezzar, raised my eyes toward heaven, and my sanity was restored. Then I praised the Most High; I honored and glorified him who lives forever. . . . Now I, Nebuchadnezzar, praise and exalt and glorify the King of heaven, because everything he does is right and all his ways are just. And those who walk in pride he is able to humble. (4:34–37)

Sanity begins with realistically evaluating oneself and God. This is exemplified in Daniel's prayer. Daniel begins with acknowledging God's righteousness and his own (with his people's) wickedness. This is sane. This is rational. This is reality. Daniel then remembers God's past great acts of redemption (9:15). He begs for mercy on the basis of the covenant between God and his people. "We do not make requests of you because we are righteous, but because of your great mercy. O Lord, listen! O Lord, forgive! O Lord, hear and act! For your sake, O my God, do not delay, because your city and your people bear your Name" (9:18–19).

Daniel identifies with God and his people. Although he was a godly, influential, and wealthy man, he pled before God in sackcloth and ashes for insight into the meaning of Jeremiah, the fate of God's people and his name. Daniel's identity was found with his people and his God. Although he was powerful and wealthy as an individual, he was not at peace or in a tranquil frame of mind. He is a picture of a man who hungers and thirsts for righteousness, for God. His identity caused him great distress, but it was the distress that accompanies sanity and godliness.

The well-being of any Christian is bound up with the well-being of the church. Perhaps the deepest insight into human personality is found at the level of the believer's identification with the community of faith. Psychological diagnostic categories often are symptoms of deeper root causes in the sphere of belief and corporate identity. Faithful preaching challenges the congregant's fundamental self-centeredness (insanity), and contrasts this with the Christ-centeredness and other-centeredness of Christian discipleship (sanity). The message of Daniel to the mature but suffering Christian is that the promise of resurrection, deliverance, and vindication is the genuine ground for hope and perseverance.

THE PRAYER OF AZARIAH

The Greek additions to Daniel include The Prayer of Azariah, which Daniel's friend prayed in the fiery furnace, and The Song of the Three Young Men, sung by the Jews, similar in form to Psalm 136.

And they walked about in the midst of the flames, singing hymns to God and blessing the Lord. Then Azariah stood and offered this prayer; in the midst of the fire he opened his mouth and said:
    "Blessed art thou, O Lord, God of our fathers,
        And worthy of praise;
        And thy name is glorified for ever.
    For thou art just in all that thou hast done to us,
        And all thy works are true and thy ways right,
        And all thy judgments are truth.
    Thou hast executed true judgments in all that
        Thou hast brought upon us
        And upon Jerusalem, the holy city of our
            fathers,
    For in truth and justice thou hast brought
        All this upon us because of our sins.
    For we have sinfully and lawlessly departed
            from thee,
        And have sinned in all things and have not
        Obeyed thy commandments;
    We have not observed them or done them,
        As thou hast commanded us that it might go
            well with us.
    So all that thou hast brought upon us,
        And all that thou hast done to us,
        Thou hast done in true judgment.
    Thou hast given us into the hands of lawless
        Enemies, most hateful rebels,

And to an unjust king, the most wicked in
all the world.
And now we cannot open our mouths;
Shame and disgrace have befallen thy
servants and worshipers.
For thy name's sake do not give us up utterly,
And do not break thy covenant,
And do not withdraw thy mercy from us,
For the sake of Abraham thy beloved
And for the sake of Isaac thy servant
And Israel thy holy one,
To whom thou didst promise
To make their descendants as many as the
stars of heaven
And as the sand on the shore of the sea.
For we, O Lord, have become fewer than any
nation,
And are brought low this day in all the world
Because of our sins.
And at this time there is no prince, or prophet,
or leader,
No burnt offering, or sacrifice, or oblation,
or incense,
No place to make an offering before thee or
to find mercy.
Yet with a contrite heart and a humble spirit
May we be accepted,
As though it were with burnt offerings of rams
and bulls,
And with tens of thousands of fat lambs;
Such may our sacrifice be in thy sight this day,
And may we wholly follow thee,
For there will be no shame for those who
trust in thee.
And now with all our heart we follow thee,
We fear thee and seek thy face.

Do not put us to shame,
>But deal with us in thy forbearance
>And in thy abundant mercy.
Deliver us in accordance with thy marvelous
>works,
>And give glory to thy name, O Lord!
Let all who do harm to thy servants be put to
>shame;
>Let them be disgraced and deprived of all
>power and dominion,
>And let their strength be broken.
Let them know that thou art the Lord, the only
>God,
>Glorious over the whole world."

Now the king's servants who threw them in did not cease feeding the furnace fires with naphtha, pitch, tow, and brush. And the flame streamed out above the furnace forty-nine cubits, and it broke through and burned those of the Chaldeans whom it caught about the furnace. But the angel of the Lord came down into the furnace to be with Azariah and his companions, and drove the fiery flame out of the furnace, and made the midst of the furnace like a moist whistling wind, so that the fire did not touch them at all or hurt or trouble them.

This bears striking similarity to the prayer of Daniel in chapter 9. Both seem cut from the same cloth, and Azariah's language seems borrowed from Daniel. Since Azariah's prayer bears such affinity with Daniel's, it is also in tension with the rest of Daniel and offers an almost entirely different perspective than elsewhere in Daniel. The prayer is reflective of the need to fill in the gaps—such as discussed in the treatment of Daniel 5. Another example of reader-response interpretation that can be seen in Azariah's prayer is the propensity to embellishment. The reader learns what fuel was used for the fire, how far the flames extended from the furnace, what it sounded like, and so on.

The prayer also exhibits an unfriendly attitude towards Nebuchadnezzar: "Thou hast given us into the hands of lawless enemies, most hateful rebels, and to an unjust king, the most wicked in all the world." This attitude toward foreign monarchs is at home in later centuries after the exile, such as in the books of Maccabees, but is not characteristic of the book of Daniel. One of the arguments for the early date of Daniel is its friendly attitude—and this aspect of Daniel is unlike the prayer of Azariah.

The additions to Daniel illustrate how the community of faith appropriated and cherished the book of Daniel in the centuries to follow, as they passed through the eras of the ram to the goat and beyond. Azariah's prayer, like Daniel's, invites the reader to participate in the distressing experience. Persecutions will come. "But as for you, the LORD took you and brought you out of the iron-smelting furnace, out of Egypt, to be the people of his inheritance, as you now are" (Deut. 4:20). Egypt was a fiery furnace. "When you pass through the waters I will be with you; and through the rivers, they shall not overwhelm you; when you walk through fire you shall not be burned, and the flame shall not consume you" (Isa. 43:2 RSV).

> Beloved, do not be surprised at the fiery ordeal which comes upon you to prove you, as though something strange were happening to you. But rejoice in so far as you share Christ's sufferings, that you may also rejoice and be glad when his glory is revealed. If you are reproached for the name of Christ, you are blessed, because the spirit of glory and of God rests upon you. (1 Peter 4:12–14 RSV)

When a Christian suffers a fiery ordeal, the book of Daniel has this message: you do not suffer alone, and you can trust Yahweh with a whole heart through it. Jesus also endured suffering and died—and yet was vindicated in the end through his resurrection. If you suffer with him and for his sake, you will also be vindicated and rewarded—with eternal life.

FOR FURTHER REFLECTION

1. How do you pray? Can you confess the sins of your people?
2. In what ways do you rejoice with those who rejoice and grieve with those who grieve?
3. What moves you to strong emotion? Does the suffering of the saints around the world cause you great distress? Why or why not?

13

THE HANDWRITING
ON THE SCROLL

D aniel 9 begins with Daniel's prayer, the one place where redemptive themes common throughout Scripture are explicitly put forward in the book. But after this prayer the chapter continues in a quite different vein, speaking cryptically of future events. In contrast to Daniel's prayer, Gabriel reasserts sapiential terminology such as *bin* ("understanding") and *sakal* ("wise").

> While I was still in prayer, Gabriel, the man I had seen in the earlier vision, came to me in swift flight about the time of the evening sacrifice. He instructed me and said to me, "Daniel, I have now come to give you insight and understanding. As soon as you began to pray, an answer was given, which I have come to tell you, for you are highly esteemed. Therefore, consider the message and understand the vision. (Dan. 9:21–23)

Gabriel is about to explain to Daniel the meaning of the vision, or revelation. But what vision? Daniel had just been praying and reading Jeremiah, not receiving a new revelation. If the vision is what follows, then Daniel receives both the mystery and the interpretation all at once. But Gabriel seems to be speaking of a vision that Daniel had already received—and the pattern in the book is that first the *raz* is revealed and then the *pesher*.

Chapter 9 begins,

> In the first year of Darius son of Xerxes (a Mede by descent), who was made ruler over the Babylonian kingdom—in the first year of his reign, I, Daniel, understood from the Scriptures, according to the word of the LORD given to Jeremiah the prophet, that the desolation of Jerusalem would last seventy years. So I turned to the Lord God and pleaded with him in prayer and petition, in fasting, and in sackcloth and ashes. (9:1–3)

After Daniel's prayer Gabriel came to explain the *raz*—which is the book of Jeremiah! The *raz* is what Daniel read in Jeremiah's prophecy—the desolation of Jerusalem would last seventy years. Daniel understood the word on some level (9:2), but Gabriel arrived so that Daniel could more fully understand it! Belteshazzar (Daniel) needed help to understand the handwriting on the scroll just as Belshazzar needed help to understand the handwriting on the wall.

THE *RAZ* ON THE SCROLL

This is Jeremiah's prophecy:

Therefore the LORD Almighty says this: "Because you have not listened to my words, I will summon all the peoples of the north and my servant Nebuchadnezzar king of Babylon," declares the LORD, "and I will bring them against this land and its inhabitants and against all the surrounding nations. I will completely destroy them and make them an object of horror and scorn, and an everlasting ruin. I will banish from them the sounds of joy and gladness, the voices of bride and bridegroom, the sound of millstones and the light of the lamp. This whole country will become a desolate wasteland, and these nations will serve the king of Babylon seventy years. But when the seventy years are fulfilled, I will punish the king of Babylon and his nation, the land of the Babylonians, for their guilt," declares the LORD, "and will make it desolate forever." (Jer. 25:8–12)

This is what the LORD says: "When seventy years are completed for Babylon, I will come to you and fulfill my gracious promise to bring you back to this place. For I know the plans I have for you," declares the LORD, "plans to prosper you and not to harm you, plans to give you hope and a future. Then you will call upon me and come and pray to me, and I will listen to you. You will seek me and find me when you seek me with all your heart. I will be found by you," declares the LORD, "and will bring you back from captivity. I will gather you from all the nations and places where I have banished you," declares the LORD, "and will bring you back to the place from which I carried you into exile." (Jer. 29:10–14)

According to Jeremiah, Nebuchadnezzar will take the Jews captive for seventy years. They will seek Yahweh with all their heart, and he will restore them. This revelation is the mystery for which Daniel requires interpretation. Gabriel is dispatched to explain it. Without heavenly assistance, Jeremiah would be as cryptic and unintelligible as the handwriting on the wall.

This is Gabriel's *pesher*:

> Seventy "sevens" are decreed for your people and your holy city to finish transgression, to put an end to sin, to atone for wickedness, to bring in everlasting righteousness, to seal up vision and prophecy and to anoint the most holy. (Dan. 9:24)

Seventy weeks of years are decreed, or 490 years. It seems as though Gabriel counts only sabbatical years, so seventy becomes seven times seventy years. After this, Jeremiah says the captives will return home. Gabriel says this means that at the end of 490 years, transgression will be finished, sin ended, wickedness atoned, everlasting righteousness come, prophecy sealed, and the most holy anointed. As usual in Daniel, the *pesher* raises more questions than the *raz*.

There are three general explanations of Gabriel's explanation of Jeremiah. Critical views argue that this is about Antiochus's transgression and sin being finished and ended. Atonement would be made for his wickedness, a true Yahweh-worshipping state would be established, the visions of Daniel would be sealed (completed) by this, and the temple Antiochus had desecrated would be anointed again. This is what Judas Maccabeus accomplished, culminating with the Hasmonean dynasty, and this is what chapter 11 of Daniel seems also to assert. Along with this argument is the corollary that this portion of Daniel was written in the second century B.C. during these events.

A second view is that Gabriel (who announced the fulfillment of these things to Mary) is here foretelling what Christ would accomplish—his sacrificial death and events culminating in the destruction of the temple. Jesus is God's last word; in the past God spoke through prophets but now through his Son. He fulfilled everything the sanctuary represented. He made atonement for all sin—there is no need for another, ever. All of God's promises are Yes, Amen in him. So Gabriel is speaking of Christ's finished work on the cross and what followed.

A third view is that Gabriel speaks of all God's purposes in history, beginning with Christ's first advent and culminating with his second coming. So the things Gabriel foretells have not been accomplished with finality yet.

Gabriel drew out of Jeremiah's prophecy the figure of 490 years and added these details:

> Know and understand this: From the issuing of the decree to restore and rebuild Jerusalem until the Anointed One, the ruler, comes, there will be seven "sevens," and sixty-two "sevens." It will be rebuilt with streets and a trench, but in times of trouble. After the sixty-two "sevens," the Anointed One will be cut off and will have nothing. The people of the ruler who will come will destroy the city and the sanctuary. The end will come like a flood: War will continue until the end, and desolations have been decreed. He will confirm a covenant with many for one "seven." In the middle of the "seven" he will put an end to sacrifice and offering. And on a wing of the temple he will set up an abomination that causes desolation, until the end that is decreed is poured out on him. (Dan. 9:25–27)

From Cyrus's decree until the Anointed One will be first 7 sevens, then 62 sevens, for a total of 69 sevens. After 69 sevens, the Anointed One will be cut off and have nothing; the people of the ruler will destroy the city and the sanctuary. For 1 seven he will confirm a covenant, but halfway into that last seven he will put an end to sacrifice and offering and set up an abomination that causes desolation. By the end of that seven, and thus of all 70 sevens, transgression and sin will be finished, atonement made, prophecy sealed, the sanctuary anointed, and everlasting righteousness established. But who is the ruler of the "people of the ruler"? Who "will confirm a covenant with many"? And who is the Anointed One?

DO THE MATH

Jeremiah wrote in 605 B.C. Jerusalem was destroyed in 586 B.C. Cyrus issued the decree to rebuild Jerusalem in 539 B.C. The Maccabees turned the tide in 165 B.C. Christ's death and resurrection was in A.D. 30 or 33. The second temple was destroyed in A.D. 70. Between Cyrus's decree and A.D. 33 are 572 years (see figure 9). But 69 sevens equal 483 years. Are Gabriel's calculations off? There are a number of ways to do the math, seven of which we will examine.

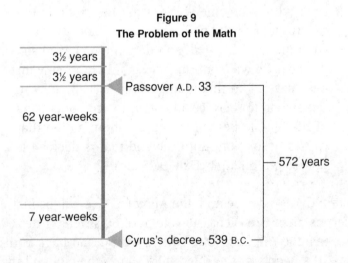

Figure 9
The Problem of the Math

3½ years

3½ years

Passover A.D. 33

62 year-weeks

572 years

7 year-weeks

Cyrus's decree, 539 B.C.

The first calculation is described in detail by Harold Hoehner;[1] one may call it the dispensational view. Cyrus's decree to rebuild the temple was in 539 B.C., but the decree to rebuild the *city* was Artaxerxes' in 444 B.C. From Nisan

1, 444 B.C., to Nisan 1, A.D. 33, there are 476 years of 365 days, or 173,740 days. From March 4 (Nisan 1) to March 29 (Passover), there are 24 more days. Add to this 116 days for leap years, and the total number of actual days between the decree to rebuild Jerusalem and Christ's death is 173,880 days. After this comes an undefined gap of time, a break in the prophecy, until the final last week, which is described in more detail in the book of Revelation. Gabriel spoke of 69 year-weeks, or 483 years. Using a stylized prophetic 360-day year, this multiplies out to 483 x 360 = 173,880, the exact same number of days that actually occurred between Artaxerxes' decree and Christ's atoning death. Thus, Gabriel exactly—to the day—predicted when Jesus would be crucified. In this view, the prince who imposes a deal (covenant) is the Antichrist. This calculation is shown in figure 10.

Figure 10
The Dispensational View

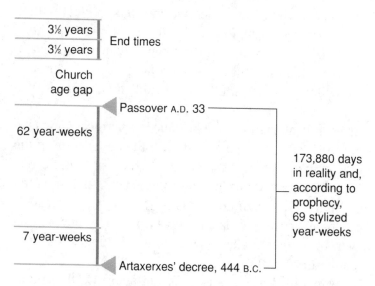

There are weaknesses with this analysis. The last seven follows a vast gap of time—but Gabriel did not suggest such an excursus between the sixty-ninth and seventieth year-week. Cyrus did in fact issue a decree to rebuild Jerusalem (Isa. 44:28; 2 Chron. 36; Ezra 1; 5:17), so the dispensational timetable needlessly waits until a hundred years after Daniel to begin! The number of days does not match unless transformed from 365 to 360 per year—would Daniel have understood it this way? Did Christ really die in A.D. 33? On what day did Artaxerxes really issue his decree? One gets the impression that the beginning and ending points are juggled to make the numbers come out right. A paraphrase of this analysis follows:

> From the issuing of Artaxerxes' decree to rebuild Jerusalem until the Lord Jesus Christ comes will be 69 sevens of 360-day years. Jerusalem's wall and the city will be rebuilt. Afterwards Jesus will be abandoned by his disciples and crucified. The troops of Titus in A.D. 70 will destroy Jerusalem and the temple once and for all. War will continue until the end times, when the Antichrist will make a deal with Jewish believers in Christ, but after three years he will betray them; and the temple, which will have been rebuilt, will once again be destroyed. Christ will then return and begin his millennial reign.

A second calculation may be called the critical view (see figure 11). Countdown begins with the destruction of the first temple. Almost 49 years later, Cyrus issues his decree. Onias III is deposed as high priest in 171 B.C. (the Anointed One cut off), and Antiochus is the prince who imposes a covenant. Seven years later, temple worship resumed. However, 62 sevens make 434 years, much longer than the required 370 years.

A modified calculus is shown in figure 12, the countdown beginning when Jeremiah wrote his prophecy. Between Jeremiah's writing his prophecy and Cyrus's ascension is a period of 47 years. Perhaps the starting point is a year earlier when Jeremiah prophesied Jerusalem's restoration, and the ending point 49 years later when Joshua was anointed as high priest. Between the writing of Jeremiah's prophecy and Onias's death is a period of 434 years, or 62 x 7. Either Daniel is somewhat confused

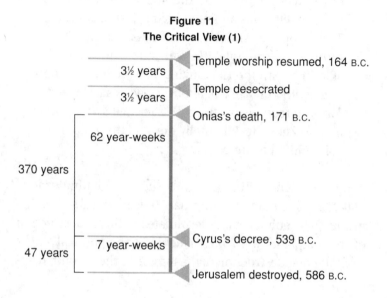

Figure 11
The Critical View (1)

3½ years — Temple worship resumed, 164 B.C.

3½ years — Temple desecrated

Onias's death, 171 B.C.

62 year-weeks

370 years

7 year-weeks — Cyrus's decree, 539 B.C.

47 years

Jerusalem destroyed, 586 B.C.

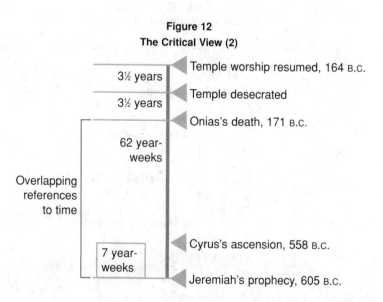

Figure 12
The Critical View (2)

3½ years — Temple worship resumed, 164 B.C.

3½ years — Temple desecrated

Onias's death, 171 B.C.

62 year-weeks

Overlapping references to time

7 year-weeks — Cyrus's ascension, 558 B.C.

Jeremiah's prophecy, 605 B.C.

about his dates, or there is an overlap of the 7 sevens and the 62 sevens, or both.

A paraphrase of the two critical analyses follows:

> From the time when Jerusalem was destroyed until Cyrus will be 49 years, and 434 years until Onias, the one who was anointed high priest, is murdered. The troops of Antiochus will massacre many and plunder the temple. He will come to an under-standing with the Hellenizing Jews, who will cooperate with him. He will abolish Jewish sacrifices and forbid circumcision. He will sacrifice swine on an altar to Zeus. He will finally die, and the temple worship will be resumed.

A fourth calculation is that of Josephus, totaling exactly 490 years, including the original 70 years in exile (see figure 13).[2] Josephus's math terminates with the destruction of the temple in A.D. 70. He calculates the political stages from the first destruction of the temple to the second, pass-

Figure 13
The View of Josephus

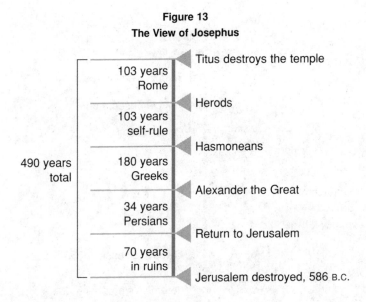

103 years Rome	Titus destroys the temple
103 years self-rule	Herods
180 years Greeks	Hasmoneans
34 years Persians	Alexander the Great
70 years in ruins	Return to Jerusalem
	Jerusalem destroyed, 586 B.C.

490 years total

ing through all four eras of the dream-statue. However, his history is very inaccurate. From 586 B.C. to A.D. 70 is 656 years. By this reckoning, Daniel is quite mistaken in his predictions.

Each of these four analyses interprets Gabriel's prophecy as a literal number of years. Thus the dispensational and critical views share with Josephus a literalistic hermeneutic when handling apocalyptic. But the book of Daniel does not lend itself to such an interpretation—especially with the examples of the handwriting on the wall and the cryptic meaning offered from Jeremiah's seemingly straightforward prophecy. Also, these four calculations begin with the supposed end-point and work backwards, finding odd starting-points such as the date of Jeremiah's writing or Artaxerxes' decree. Rather than starting at an assumed end-point and counting backwards, the following views start at a beginning-point and count forwards— while not expecting a literalistic meaning. Gabriel says that there will be 70 sevens more after Jeremiah's prophecy ends; this begins with Cyrus's decree in 539 B.C.

C. F. Keil reads Gabriel's time frame symbolically.[3] After 49 years comes the Jubilee (Lev. 25:8–12). Forty-nine years constitute a Sabbath of Sabbaths (see figure 14). Gabriel's "seven 'sevens' " is an indefinite period which symbolically culminates with a Jubilee. The first 49 years represent the time from Cyrus's redemptive decree to Christ's coming. The following 62 year-weeks is an indefinite period of the church age—an extended Jubilee. The seventieth week features an evil prince who offers a covenant and is cut off—this is the Antichrist. The eschaton culminates the seventieth week, followed by a tenth Jubilee, Christ's second advent. Thus, some of the expected events (making an end of sin, ushering in everlasting righteousness, etc.) await the eschaton. A paraphrase of Keil's view would read as follows:

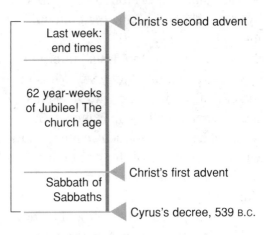

Figure 14
C. F. Keil's View

Christ's second advent

Last week: end times

62 year-weeks of Jubilee! The church age

Christ's first advent

Sabbath of Sabbaths

Cyrus's decree, 539 B.C.

From the issuing of Cyrus's decree in 539 B.C. to the coming of Jesus will be an indefinite period of time, followed by the Jubilee. Jerusalem will be rebuilt so that it takes in a wide space ("trench" in 9:25 is not a good translation) symbolically, meaning that the spread of the gospel will continue throughout the world for an indefinite period of time, a symbolic 62 weeks of years. To the end there will be wars, for God irrevocably determines desolations. In the last symbolic week, the Messiah will lose his place and function as Messiah ("the Anointed One will be cut off"). An ungodly prince will impose on the mass of the people a strong covenant that they should follow him and give themselves to him as their god. On the wings of abomination he comes desolating, until the destruction decreed by God will pour down on him like a flood, ushering in the tenth and final Jubilee, the consummation of all things.

Meredith Kline and E. J. Young offer two variations on a sixth calculation. Like Keil, Kline also reckons a Jubilee following the first 49 years, but the tenth Jubilee is the antitypical Jubilee, the final state in eternity that lasts forever. He argues that the prophecy is concerned with God's covenant with Israel, especially its consummation. After all, Gabriel's prophecy follows Daniel's prayer, which invokes the covenant. Seventy year-weeks are a series of ten Jubilees culminating in the proclamation of deliverance, atonement, vengeance, and the establishment of God's covenant with his people. The prince who comes in is Christ, the risen and exalted Lord of history, who sovereignly and providentially supervises the destruction of the apostate temple.[4] This is shown graphically in figure 15.

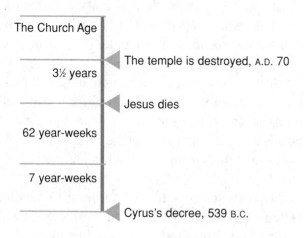

Figure 15
The View of Meredith Kline and E. J. Young

The Church Age

The temple is destroyed, A.D. 70

3½ years

Jesus dies

62 year-weeks

7 year-weeks

Cyrus's decree, 539 B.C.

A paraphrase of Gabriel's words according to Kline's analysis follows:

> Gabriel's words are about the fate of the covenant, which Daniel saw in Jeremiah and prayed about. The Messiah would come in and die, thus establishing a new covenant in his blood and bringing the old to its conclusion. The temple would be restored, but then defiled. The Messiah would sovereignly and

providentially cause it to be destroyed a final time, since it would no longer be needed after he had made atonement for sin.

Thus the church is now in the second half of the last week of the seventy, and the end is very near at hand. The book of Revelation also presents the church's experience in the wilderness, persecuted, witnessing, trampled upon, in a city allegorically called Sodom, which is also Jerusalem, in a time frame of 3 1/2 years (Rev. 11:1–12; 12:1–6, 13–14).

A variation of this calculation is Young's, who argues that the 70 years start with Cyrus's decree and end with the destruction of the temple under Titus, the prince who comes in.[5] Christ himself is the prince who makes a covenant—a new covenant with his people. The last act of redemptive history is the destruction of the temple. This can be seen in Jesus' own interpretation in Matthew 24:1–30 and Luke 21:5–24. Just as the general resurrection of the just and the unjust at the end of time begins with Christ's resurrection as the first fruits, so also the final judgment at the end of time begins with the destruction of the temple in Jerusalem. A paraphrase of this view might read as follows:

> From Cyrus's decree until the Lord Jesus Christ dies is 69 sevens. General Titus Flavius Vespasianus will destroy the temple, and Jesus will institute a new covenant. As Sinclair Ferguson summarizes, "Within four decades from the Messiah's rejection, the soil on which the Temple was built, so beloved by Daniel, would once again be defiled by pagans. Jerusalem would again be desolate."[6]

Perhaps it is a sign of the end times when scholars disagree on whether it is the Christ or the Antichrist spoken about in a text! According to Kline, Gabriel meant that the temple's destruction was a good thing (Jesus uses it as a springboard to found the new covenant)—but would Daniel or any Jew have understood it this way? Titus destroyed it; perhaps this is the last stage of redemptive history. But if Christ is the Prince mentioned at first, then Gabriel speaks of two princes, Christ and Titus. And Christians have been living in the last half of the final seven years since A.D. 70. But this reckoning ignores the precise dating of Christ's death that the dispensationalists calculated. The critics assume Daniel is wrong; if he is not, they must strain the text (overlapping the sevens). A hostile government can disrupt church services, but does this constitute Christ being cut off? Is Keil reading allegorically when he identifies Jerusalem with the church? And do the non-literalists who see the final week in the end-times claim, along with the dispensationalists, that the temple will be rebuilt? Figure 16 is a synopsis of the seven views, originally compiled by the late Ray Dillard, and then embellished by the author.

Figure 16
Seven Calculations of the Seventy Sevens

	70–7s		Start				End			Prince who comes in				Prince who imposes covenant		
	Literal	Figurative	605 B.C.	586 B.C.	539 B.C.	444 B.C.	165 B.C.	A.D. 70	Eschaton	Antiochus	Titus	Christ	Antichrist	Antiochus	Christ	Antichrist
Dispensational	✓					✓			✓				✓			
Critical 1	✓		✓				✓			✓				✓		
Critical 2	✓				✓		✓			✓				✓		
Josephus	✓				✓		✓			✓						
Keil		✓		✓					✓			✓				✓
Kline[1]		✓		✓			✓					✓			✓	
Young[1]		✓		✓			✓					✓			✓	

1. The second half of the last seven terminates in the eschaton.

Sometimes one brings one's *pesher* to the text—and this is true of the calculations above. Meaning is generated by the reader in these cases, it is not really found in Gabriel's words. Tremper Longman offers still another "calculation" that considers the failure of the various attempts to make specific connections between the seventy weeks and events of history.[7] He cannot identify the Prince, the Anointed One, and so on. Gabriel merely confirms what is taught in the rest of Daniel—the saints of God will suffer until the end, and only God knows the time of the end. Faithful living before God in these times leads to restoration—and ultimately eternal life—while the oppressor will certainly be judged according to God's unrevealed timetable. The text is written specifically to confound any attempt to interpret with more specificity. This author is most comfortable with that approach, although he likes to think of himself as living in the last half of the seventieth week!

JESUS AND HIS GOSPEL

Gabriel's interpretation of Jeremiah stretches far beyond the restoration of the Jews after the exile, and has in view the coming of Christ and the satisfaction of God's justice (which will finish transgression, put an end to sin, atone for wickedness, bring in everlasting righteousness, seal up vision and prophecy, and anoint the most holy). Gabriel makes clear that Jeremiah's prophecy is all about Jesus—prophecy stretches and yearns towards Christ and the consummation of all things. Here in chapter 9 this is abundantly clear. Figure 17 is a reprise of Patterson's chart shown earlier (p. 118). Note the summation of Keil's analysis under chapter 9.

This helps identify the scope of Daniel's book and the centrality of the Christ in it. The great Rock that grows and fills the earth, the son of man's reception of the kingdom,

Figure 17
The Kingdoms and Symbols of Daniel

Chapter	2	7	8	9 (Keil)	10–12
Babylon	Golden head	Winged lion			
Medo-Persia	Silver chest	Bear on its side	Ram	Decree to rebuild;	Four kings
Greece	Bronze belly	Leopard with four wings and heads	Goat	7 sevens; Anointed One	Mighty king + successors
Antiochus			Little horn		King of the North
Rome	Iron legs, clay toes	Dreadful beast		62 sevens	
Last evil king		Little horn		1 seven	Willful king
Final kingdom	Rock	Son of man		The End	Resurrection, felicity

the resurrection at the end of history, all happen when transgression and sin is finished, atonement is made for wickedness, everlasting righteousness brought in, and the most holy anointed. In chapter 9, some see the Antichrist; in chapter 11 there is a willful king, and a little horn in chapter 7. But the outworking of all these matters begins and ends with Christ.

FOR FURTHER REFLECTION

1. Where do you go for counsel when you are distressed or confused?
2. Jesus will usher in the end of the world and the vindication of the saints. How does this fact change the way you deal with stress and disappointment?
3. Where on God's timetable are we now? How soon will it be until Jesus returns?

I4

WAR IN HEAVEN

Daniel 10 reveals celestial realities behind the terrestrial events delineated in the next vision—thus serving as prologue to the rest of the book. In fact, the word *'emet* ("true, truth") opens (10:1) and closes (10:21) the chapter, a poetic device called *inclusion*. This in turn forms a bridge with Dan 11:2 and the subsequent chapter, which traces the earthly analog to the heavenly.

WHO IS STRONG, WHO IS WEAK, AND WHO IS LIKE GOD

In chapter 10 there is a repeated motif of Daniel's personal weakness. Daniel mourned for three "weeks of days" (10:2), as distinguished from the year-weeks of chapter 9. He refused good food and normal grooming. When the answer came, those with him trembled and fled. In Daniel 10:8, there "did not remain in me *koh* [power]" (used in Dan. 1:4 of the "ability" to stand before the king). In verses 9–11, he swoons, shakes, and trembles: "I turned my face toward the ground and was dumb" (10:15 RSV); "Pains have come upon me, and I retain no *koh*" (10:16 RSV); "No strength remains in me, and no breath is left in me" (10:17 RSV). Daniel is a pitiful weakling. Of course, in the next vision it is the saints who are weak and needy.

In Daniel 10:4–6, this is contrasted with the radiant splendor and glory of the one in the vision. He is a heavenly warrior bristling with power who strengthens Daniel with a touch. He is Daniel's opposite. Although not named, elsewhere in the book (8:16; 9:21) the angel who ministers to Daniel is called Gabriel, which means "warrior of God." The name itself exudes strength. He calms Daniel and assures him that his petitions have been heard from the time he began to pray—but Gabriel has been hindered in coming because of the cosmic battle waged in the realms beyond human ken.

Gabriel appeared to Daniel, but was beyond description. He reflected the glory of God such that humans trembled and fled. His description is reminiscent of Ezekiel 1:26–28:

> And above the firmament over their heads there was the likeness of a throne, in appearance like sapphire; and seated above the likeness of a throne was a likeness as it were of a human form. And upward from what had the appearance of his loins I saw as it were gleaming bronze, like the appearance of fire enclosed round about; and downward from what had the appearance of his loins I saw as it were the appearance of fire, and there was brightness round about him. Like the appearance of the bow that is in the cloud on the day of rain, so was the appearance of the brightness round about. Such was the appearance of the likeness of the glory of the LORD. And when I saw it, I fell upon my face, and I heard the voice of one speaking. (RSV)

See also Revelation 1:12–16:

> Then I turned to see the voice that was speaking to me, and on turning I saw seven golden lampstands, and in the midst of the lampstands one like a son of man, clothed with a long robe and with a golden girdle round his breast; his head and his hair were white as white wool, white as snow; his eyes were like a flame of fire, his feet were like burnished bronze, refined as in a furnace, and his voice was like the sound of many waters; in his right hand he held seven stars, from his mouth issued a sharp two-edged sword, and his face was like the sun shining in full strength. (RSV)

This last description is of Jesus, the incarnate glory of God. Ezekiel describes the divine glory that overwhelms the prophet and overloads his senses. This is reminiscent of the Israelites at Sinai, trembling with fear at the mountain's foot, afraid to approach lest they die. Gabriel is not God, but he reflects such godlike resplendence that in comparison to him, all humanity is weak and helpless. If Gabriel could not overcome the forces arrayed against him, how could Daniel, or even all Israel, hope to stand?

While Daniel prayed, humbled himself, and mourned for twenty-one days, the prince of Persia resisted Gabriel until Michael arrived. Leaving Michael to dispatch the prince, Gabriel at last reached Daniel to comfort and inform him concerning these matters.

Although Calvin identified the prince with an earthly figure known to history (Cambyses), today he is identified as a spiritual enemy. Joyce Baldwin calls him "a representative of Persia in the heavenlies"; Tremper Longman, "a supernatural being who fights on behalf of that human kingdom"; James Montgomery calls this "war in heaven." Elsewhere in Scripture there are a few indications of a theology of demonic forces that identify with human civilizations such as Persia. One is Deuteronomy 32:8–9, where the Septuagint translation agrees with the Dead Sea Scrolls to read,

> When the Most High gave to the nations their
>   inheritance,
> when he separated the sons of men,
> he fixed the bounds of the peoples
> according to the number of the sons of God.
> For the LORD's portion is his people,
> Jacob his allotted heritage.

Our Hebrew Bible reads, "according to the sons of Israel." It is easier to imagine a scribe modifying "God" to "Israel" in this case than the reverse. If the Septuagint and the Dead Sea Scrolls preserve an earlier reading, then here the "sons of God"—that is, angelic beings—are assigned to different ethnic groups. This is an example of divine election—Yahweh chooses a people for himself, and the rest of humanity are relegated to various supernatural beings, until the day when the strong man's house is plundered and the nations are no longer deceived (Luke 11:19–22; Rev. 20:1–3). Deuteronomy 4:19 speaks of the host of heaven allotted to the peoples. Perhaps Isaiah 24:21–23 speaks of these hosts as being punished along with their earthly counterparts, the kings of the earth.

The conflict is not against flesh and blood, but against principalities, powers, spiritual hosts of wickedness in the heavenly realms. In Jesus' day the Jews' enemy was not really Rome, although they refused to see this. Both the Jews and Rome were in thrall to Satan, sin, and death. Jesus battled with these principalities and powers, and set his people free from their bondage. But this conflict raged long before the Word became flesh. Jesus the Son of Man is the champion in the Gospels; Michael is the champion in the book of Daniel.

Gabriel said to Daniel that no one was strong with him except Michael. Michael is called "the great prince who protects your people" (12:1). His name means, "Who is like God." In Jude 9, Michael is called the "archangel" who disputed with the devil. He also appears in Revelation 12:7–11:

And there was war in heaven. Michael and his angels fought against the dragon, and the dragon and his angels fought back. But he was not strong enough, and they lost their place in heaven. The great dragon was hurled down—that ancient serpent called the devil, or Satan, who leads the whole world astray. He was hurled to the earth, and his angels with him.
Then I heard a loud voice in heaven say:

"Now have come the salvation and the power
        and the kingdom of our God,
    and the authority of his Christ.
For the accuser of our brothers,
    who accuses them before our God day and
        night,
    has been hurled down.
They overcame him
    by the blood of the Lamb
    and by the word of their testimony;
they did not love their lives so much
    as to shrink from death."

Michael and his angels defeat Satan by the blood of the Lamb. The decisive heavenly triumph of Michael was secured by Jesus' shed blood. "For the Lord himself will come down from heaven, with a loud command, with the voice of the archangel" (1 Thess. 4:16). "Archangel" means "chief angel," the captain of the Lord's armies. Perhaps this Michael is the Angel of Yahweh, the second person of the Trinity. "Who is like God" is his name; possibly also "one like a son of man"—come to receive the kingdom after the wars of heaven and earth are won. In any case, Michael is the warrior who fights for Israel; he is Israel's Prince, just as Persia and Greece have their angelic counterparts.

WHAT IS THE TRUE *RAZ*; WHAT IS THE TRUE *PESHER*?

The great mystery in Daniel (or anywhere else) is not the meaning of visions and dreams; the great mystery that requires interpretation is real life. The dreams and visions are interpretations of life. They provide larger-than-life pictures of reality that interpret reality. Describing a homicidal, utterly vicious, monstrous goat, which through sheer brutish might grinds a horrendous ram into the ground, is much more emotionally potent than a detailed chronicle of the exploits of Alexander the Great against the Persian Empire. The rise and fall of empires are supplied images that redefine them for the believer. History is the *raz*; the images of the dreams are the *pesher*.

In chapter 2, great empires are lifeless like a statue, and their worshippers as programmed and mindless as the empires. In chapter 7, the nations are raving brutes and inhuman monstrosities. Despite their claims and aspirations, they are not autonomous, but wield derivative authority—finally judged by the Ancient of Days. Apocalyptic literature insists that reality is the invisible forces working behind the scenes, more clearly perceived in dreams and visions than in history books. Chapter 10 is also interpreting, giving meaning and insight into, the events of history—events limned in the next chapter.

Chapter 10 highlights Daniel's personal weakness and powerlessness. Israel is also impotent and helpless before great powers. Persia dominates the Jews, and in chapter 11, the incoming Greek kingdom will be more terrible. These forces buffet and wear out the saints. Their power consists in their heavenly administration, the spiritual host that directs and characterizes each nation. The powerful prince of Persia resists Gabriel, and after that, the prince of Greece will arise. The ram rages; the goat is mad with power.

The great nations that dominate puny Israel have powerful spiritual forces behind them that supernaturally give them strength, purpose, and victory. But what does little Israel have? Some Lilliputian flunky who cannot hold his own? No! Israel has Michael the archangel, captain of the hosts of Yahweh, the one who will throw down the dragon from heaven. The celestial realm looks very different from the terrestrial. Although Israel is weak and small, her angel is great and powerful. The spirits of the nations cannot stand before him. Therefore, Israel is assured of victory! This is why the Jews were allowed to return to their homeland and rebuild their temple—because Gabriel confirmed and strengthened Darius (11:1). Spiritually, Israel conquered Persia, and will surely conquer Greece as well.

This surely does "re-image" their situation. Gabriel strengthened Daniel—and all Israel. Daniel was ill for three sevens of days, echoing Israel's eschatological time parsed into sevens of years. Israel will face terrible and difficult year-weeks (as Daniel mourned for three sevens), but in a sphere that cannot be seen, they are winning great victories.

Christians also struggle against principalities and powers. Michael still fights on behalf of the church. Satan has been defeated by those who did not love their lives so much that they shrank from death—as the Lamb of God shed his blood for his saints (Rev. 12). While we wait for Jesus to return with the archangel's call, to receive us into the clouds to be forever with him, we attend to prayer, faithfully keeping his word, proclaiming his gospel throughout the world, and thus delivering the lost from their invisible bondage to sin and Satan.

Amen, come, Lord Jesus!

FOR FURTHER REFLECTION

1. When do you feel powerless or helpless? What do you do in those times? What *can* you do?
2. What are the big issues you struggle with? Are these the true big issues?
3. What is the real cosmic struggle in life?
4. Christians are told to put on the full armor of God to withstand the devil's wiles (Eph. 6:10–18). How do you participate in this cosmic struggle?
5. How has Jesus defeated the enemy in this spiritual conflict (Col. 2:15)?

15

WAR ON EARTH

Daniel 11:1–12:4 shows the earthly analog to the spiritual realities of chapter 10. Terrestrial events are foretold from the Persian period (the ram of chap. 8) to the Greek period (the goat). The Greek period is sketched with enough detail to recognize—after the fact—that God's calendar is on track. As the events transpire, the Jews can be confident as boastful horns rear up and utter great things against heaven. However, the future is not revealed in such a way that the Jews can predict who or what will happen next. It is only after the fact that the meaning of each verse becomes clear.

KNOWN HISTORY[1]

Alexander the Great quickly conquered the known world. Upon his death, the empire was apportioned to four generals (11:4). This is the fourfold quality of the flying leopard of chapter 7, and the four horns on the goat of chapter 8. Of these four generals, two were relevant to the fortunes of Israel: the Seleucid kingdom to the north (Syria), and the Ptolemaic kingdom to the south (Egypt).

These two kingdoms contested over Palestine for centuries. Figure 18 shows the successions of both kingdoms. Eleven events known are keyed by number.

> The king of the South will become strong, but one of his commanders will become even stronger than he and will rule his own kingdom with great power. After some years, they will become allies. The daughter of the king of the South will go to the king of the North to make an alliance, but she will not retain her power, and he and his power will not last. In those days she will be handed over, together with her royal escort and her father and the one who supported her. (11:5–6)

Ptolemy I of Egypt (the king of the South) was at first in control of Palestine. Seleucus I soon took possession. (1) Ptolemy later annexed Palestine. (2) In 250 B.C. Berenice, Ptolemy II Philadelphus's daughter, married Antiochus II

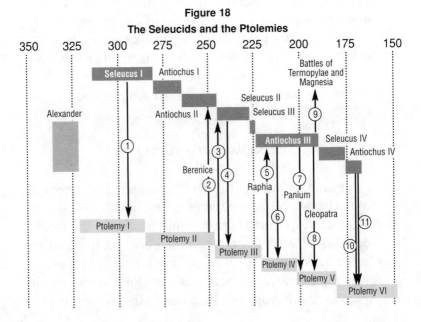

Figure 18
The Seleucids and the Ptolemies

Theos. Their son would have ruled both Syria and Egypt, but Antiochus's first wife poisoned all three of them. So that attempt at marriage alliance failed.

> One from her family line will arise to take her place. He will attack the forces of the king of the North and enter his fortress; he will fight against them and be victorious. He will also seize their gods, their metal images and their valuable articles of silver and gold and carry them off to Egypt. For some years he will leave the king of the North alone. Then the king of the North will invade the realm of the king of the South but will retreat to his own country. (11:7–9)

(3) Ptolemy III Euergetes, Berenice's brother, attacked Seleucus II and plundered Syria. (4) Seleucus retaliated and was partially successful, but Ptolemy remained in control of Egypt.

> His sons will prepare for war and assemble a great army, which will sweep on like an irresistible flood and carry the battle as far as his fortress. Then the king of the South will march out in a rage and fight against the king of the North, who will raise a large army, but it will be defeated. When the army is carried off, the king of the South will be filled with pride and will slaughter many thousands, yet he will not remain triumphant. For the king of the North will muster another army, larger than the first; and after several years, he will advance with a huge army fully equipped. (11:10–13)

The sons of Seleucus II were Seleucus III and Antiochus III the Great. (5) In 217 B.C., Ptolemy IV and Antiochus III fought the battle of Raphia where Antiochus had to retreat.

(6) Between 212 and 205 B.C. Antiochus regained much of what he had lost.

> In those times many will rise against the king of the South. The violent men among your own people will rebel in fulfillment of the vision, but without success. Then the king of the North will come and build up siege ramps and will capture a fortified city. The forces of the South will be powerless to resist; even their best troops will not have the strength to stand. The invader will do as he pleases; no one will be able to stand against him. He will establish himself in the Beautiful Land and will have the power to destroy it. (11:14–16)

(7) In 198 B.C., Antiochus the Great won the Battle of Panium, so after about a hundred years of Egyptian rule, Palestine was again in Syrian control. History was inexorably moving toward the rise of Antiochus IV Epiphanes, the little horn of chapter 8. The participation of the Jews is noted for the first time.

> He will determine to come with the might of his entire kingdom and will make an alliance with the king of the South. And he will give him a daughter in marriage in order to overthrow the kingdom, but his plans will not succeed or help him. (11:17)

(8) Again a marriage alliance was attempted to weld Egypt and Syria. Antiochus the Great gave his daughter Cleopatra to Ptolemy V Epiphanes, hoping to influence Egypt. However, she worked against him. In 182 B.C. Ptolemy died, and Cleopatra ruled Egypt until her son, Ptolemy VI, succeeded her after eight years.

Then he will turn his attention to the coastlands and will take many of them, but a commander will put an end to his insolence and will turn his insolence back upon him. After this, he will turn back toward the fortresses of his own country but will stumble and fall, to be seen no more. (11:18–19)

(9) In 196 B.C. Antiochus the Great came to the attention of the rising power of Rome when he extended his reach to Thrace. He disregarded Rome's threats until he was beaten in 191 B.C. at Thermopylae; the following year at Magnesia, Lucius Cornelius Scipio ignominiously defeated him again. He died in 187 B.C. The fact that Daniel envisions an outside power suggests that the Greek kingdom is not the final one (the legs of iron), but there is another waiting in the wings for its moment on the stage of history.

His successor will send out a tax collector to maintain the royal splendor. In a few years, however, he will be destroyed, yet not in anger or in battle. (11:20)

Seleucus IV Philopator was assassinated in 175 B.C. by a conspiracy led by Heliodorus the prime minister. His younger brother, who had been held hostage by Rome since the Battle of Magnesia, returned. His name was Antiochus IV Epiphanes.

He will be succeeded by a contemptible person who has not been given the honor of royalty. He will invade the kingdom when its people feel secure, and he will seize it through intrigue. (11:21)

Although he was not heir to the throne, Antiochus IV seized power. The contest between northern and southern kings culminated with one Syrian responsible for great suffering and persecution of the saints. This Antiochus became the paradigm of human power that exalts itself against God.

> Then an overwhelming army will be swept away before him; both it and a prince of the covenant will be destroyed. After coming to an agreement with him, he will act deceitfully, and with only a few people he will rise to power. When the richest provinces feel secure, he will invade them and will achieve what neither his fathers nor his forefathers did. He will distribute plunder, loot and wealth among his followers. He will plot the overthrow of fortresses— but only for a time. (11:22–24)

A usurper, Antiochus IV politically promoted himself, violently dealing with any opposition, even to the point of executing the legitimate high priest Onias III in 171 B.C. This Onias is thought by some to be the Anointed One cut off (9:26).

> With a large army he will stir up his strength and courage against the king of the South. The king of the South will wage war with a large and very powerful army, but he will not be able to stand because of the plots devised against him. Those who eat from the king's provisions will try to destroy him; his army will be swept away, and many will fall in battle. The two kings, with their hearts bent on evil, will sit at the same table and lie to each other, but to no avail, because an end will still come at the appointed time. The king of the North will return to his own country with great wealth, but his heart will be set against the holy covenant. He will take action against it and then return to his own country. (11:25–28)

(10) Antiochus encroached into Egypt in 170–169 B.C. He looted the temple in Jerusalem and forbade the daily sacrifice. He put an idol there, the "abomination that causes desolation." The following text from 1 Maccabees helps to detail these activities:

When Antiochus saw that his kingdom was established, he determined to become king of the land of Egypt, that he might reign over both kingdoms. So he invaded Egypt with a strong force, with chariots and elephants and cavalry and with a large fleet. He engaged Ptolemy king of Egypt in battle, and Ptolemy turned and fled before him, and many were wounded and fell. And they captured the fortified cities in the land of Egypt, and he plundered the land of Egypt.

After subduing Egypt, Antiochus returned in the one hundred and forty-third year. He went up against Israel and came to Jerusalem with a strong force. He arrogantly entered the sanctuary and took the golden altar, the lampstand for the light, and all its utensils. He took also the table for the bread of the Presence, the cups for drink offerings, the bowls, the golden censers, the curtain, the crowns, and the gold decoration on the front of the temple; he stripped it all off. He took the silver and the gold, and the costly vessels; he took also the hidden treasures which he found. Taking them all, he departed to his own land. He committed deeds of murder, and spoke with great arrogance. Israel mourned deeply in every community, rulers and elders groaned, maidens and young men became faint, the beauty of women faded. Every bridegroom took up the lament; she who sat in the bridal chamber was mourning. Even the land shook for its inhabitants, and all the house of Jacob was clothed with shame. (1 Macc. 1:16–28)

The tone and spirit of 1–2 Maccabees is hostile and unfavorable to foreign monarchs. If Daniel is a second-century document, it would hardly trace Antiochus's crimes so briefly and dispassionately. Daniel seems not emotionally vested in the period. Although the details are accurate, Daniel simply does not read like a product of second-century Judaism which had terribly suffered.

> At the appointed time he will invade the South again, but this time the outcome will be different from what it was before. Ships of the western coastlands will oppose him, and he will lose heart. Then he will turn back and vent his fury against the holy covenant. He will return and show favor to those who forsake the holy covenant. (11:29–30)

(11) Two years later, Antiochus again invaded Egypt. The Roman fleet intervened, and the proconsul Gaius Popilius Laenas of Rome confronted Antiochus with an ultimatum. Antiochus then turned his attention to Palestine, causing some Jews to forsake their God and traditions.

> His armed forces will rise up to desecrate the temple fortress and will abolish the daily sacrifice. Then they will set up the abomination that causes desolation. With flattery he will corrupt those who have violated the covenant, but the people who know their God will firmly resist him. (11:31–32)

The state always has power to persecute—and this power often separates the wheat from the chaff—those who are fully devoted to their God from those who are worshippers of convenience.

> Those who are wise will instruct many, though for a time they will fall by the sword or be burned or

captured or plundered. When they fall, they will receive a little help, and many who are not sincere will join them. Some of the wise will stumble, so that they may be refined, purified and made spotless until the time of the end, for it will still come at the appointed time. (11:33–35)

The motif of wisdom again asserts itself in the book of Daniel. Oppression is an opportunity to show forth wisdom. This is how Daniel characterizes the turmoil of this period—and this recalls the book's paradigm-setting first chapter. By Jesus' time the successors to the "wise" and to those who militarily revolted were the Sadducees and the Pharisees, under the domination of Rome and the Herods.

APOCALYPTIC TIME

From Daniel 11:36 on, the book describes events unknown to history, although consistent with the character of Antiochus IV Epiphanes. "Epiphanes" means "God-manifest." This contrasts with the figure of chapter 10, Michael, "One who is like God." Which one of these two figures is really God manifest? Which is really one like the son of God (Dan. 3:25)? For those who have seen the true Michael, counterfeits are easy to spot.

Daniel 11:40–45 describes events patently *not* consistent with known history. Antiochus did *not* again invade Egypt, there was no battle as described, and he died in Syria, not Palestine. Daniel 11:40 begins with 'et qets ("the time of the end"), apparently describing events of a later time. The phrase occurs four times in Daniel (11:35; 12:4, 9). Perhaps at this point the chapter is beginning to look much further into the future than the period of Antiochus. Daniel 12:1–4 again speaks of Michael arising, and with him will come the resurrection of the dead. When Michael rises, the last evil king will come to a sudden end, the martyred saints will return to life, and the ultimate reversal, the ultimate vindication, will take place.

In Luke 21:20–33 Jesus connects the destruction of the temple in A.D. 70 to the end of the world; the first stroke of judgment falls on the temple. A first-century Christian might have expected after this event that the end would come in that generation. But the temple's fall was only the beginning of the end—and so far there have been about two thousand years between that event and the end of the end. In the same way, the rivalry and wars of kings will continue until the end of the end times. This End will feature the antitype of all previous kings, the ultimate evil ruler; the one to whom penultimate little horns like Nebuchadnezzar and Darius and Antiochus Epiphanes point forward.

Antiochus is not the little horn of chapter 7, judged by the heavenly court. In chapter 11 he is not the final power, but is stymied and frustrated. The rising power in chapter 11 is Rome. On the heels of chapter 11 are the appearance of Michael, the resurrection of the dead, and the end of history—which come in the days of a final power, not the humiliated Antiochus. Daniel 11:40–45 begins, "at the time of the end," which may demarcate a new movement in the prophecy—but the king described seems to be a continuation of Antiochus's career, contending with the king of the South. There is a blurring between Antiochus and the end of the world, but this does not mean that the book of Daniel envisions Antiochus as the final king. In chapter 11, "the king of the North" is a title for no fewer than four individuals (not counting 11:40), and "the king of the South" for no fewer than six kings (see figure 19). So it is no surprise if the king of the North is not Antiochus—all of the kings of Syria and Egypt are blended together by nomenclature. However, one might ask why a future king would want to contend with the king of the South—a rivalry that has been a dead issue since the Roman Empire.

Figure 19
The Kings of the South and of the North in Daniel 11

Verse	The King of the South	The King of the North
5	Ptolemy I	
6	Ptolemy II	Antiochus II
7		Seleucus II
9	Ptolemy III	
11	Ptolemy IV	Antiochus III
14	Ptolemy V	
25	Ptolemy VI	Antiochus IV

There are three views on how to understand the final willful king. The critics argue that the writer was speaking of Antiochus and simply got it wrong. A second view is that the ancient rivalry between North and South for the possession of Palestine will literally resume. The third view sees Antiochus as a prototype of ambitious rulers and governments that arise throughout history using religion and ideology to promote themselves. Antiochus is an example of these rulers' malignity, a glimpse into the future—as patterns repeat and rulers impose their will and dominate the church. Thus the ancient contest between North and South is typical and symbolic of the kind of imperialistic ambitions future kings will exhibit—with the people of God, the church, caught in the cross-fire. Again, Patterson's table helps to clarify matters (see figure 20).

The two little horns are similar, but are not identical. The last half of the last seven years seems of one piece with the rest of the 70 year-weeks, but is actually very different. The iron legs seem to be Rome but apparently last until the

Figure 20
The Kingdoms and Symbols of Daniel

Chapter	2	7	8	9 (Keil)	10–12
Babylon	Golden head	Winged lion			
Medo-Persia	Silver chest	Bear on its side	Ram	Decree to rebuild;	Four kings
Greece	Bronze belly	Leopard with four wings and heads	Goat	7 sevens; Anointed One	Mighty king + successors
Antiochus			Little horn		King of the North
Rome	Iron legs, clay toes	Dreadful beast		62 sevens	
Last evil king		Little horn		1 seven	Willful king
Final kingdom	Rock	Son of man		The End	Resurrection, felicity

end, crushed by the kingdom of God. So there are two significant northern kings—Antiochus the little horn who simply dies like any king, and the final king, the little horn judged when the saints receive the kingdom.

IDOLATRY VERSUS THE WISE

Daniel reveals that the hubris of kings like Nebuchadnezzar and Belshazzar and Antiochus will continue until a final king like them will arise to take their God-spurning attitude to an extreme expression. This will happen when the wise teach many, but a few will stumble.

The king will do as he pleases. He will exalt and magnify himself above every god and will say unheard-of things against the God of gods. . . . He will show no regard for the gods of his fathers or for the one desired by women, nor will he regard any god, but will exalt himself above them all. (Dan. 11:36–37)

The future evil king will exalt himself above the divine. However, human beings always worship something; they cannot escape their worshipping hearts.

> Instead of them [the gods], he will honor a god of fortresses; a god unknown to his fathers he will honor with gold and silver, with precious stones and costly gifts. He will attack the mightiest fortresses with the help of a foreign god and will greatly honor those who acknowledge him. He will make them rulers over many people and will distribute the land at a price. (Dan. 11:38–39)

This future king will not "regard any god, but will exalt himself." Instead of traditional gods, he will honor a "god of fortresses." But this king does not regard any god. It is unlikely that Daniel would dignify a false god by admitting that it actually can help the king. The evidence suggests that this god is not a divine being at all, but is something like Nebuchadnezzar's golden image, like the law forbidding prayer to any but Darius.

> The "god of fortresses" is the personification of war, and the thought is this: he will regard no other god, but only war; the taking of fortresses he will make his god; and he will worship this god above all as the means of gaining the world-power. Of this god, war as the object of deification, it might be said that his fathers knew nothing, because no other king had made war his religion, his god to whom he offered up in sacrifice all, gold, silver, precious stones, jewels. . . . With the help of this god, who was unknown to his fathers, he will so proceed against the strong fortresses that he rewards with honor, might, and wealth those who acknowledge him.[2]

In the end, the hauteur of world conquerors will give rise to a monstrous kingdom with iron horns and bronze claws. Its only religion will be the making of war, coming into conflict with those who worship the Most High God and his Son—the one who fights for them and will resurrect them in the end of time.

Daniel 12:3 testifies that in this time the wise will "shine like the brightness of the heavens." Elsewhere in the Bible, the Hebrew word for "shine" means to admonish, to warn (Eccl. 4:13, "Better a poor but wise youth than an old but foolish king who no longer knows how to take *warning*"). "Brightness" is found elsewhere only in Ezekiel 8:2: "I looked, and I saw a figure like that of a man. From what appeared to be his waist down he was like fire, and from there up his appearance was as *bright* as glowing metal." The wise will shine/admonish and in doing so will image the glory of God—like the heavenly host of starry skies.

This is a summation of the book of Daniel. God's people will be subjected to hostile great powers. This oppression provides the opportunity for the wisdom of the saints to be displayed, while others seek it but cannot find it, like the Chaldeans in Nebuchadnezzar's court, until the Great Reversal when the saints will rise from the dead to receive the eternal kingdom. They will shine like stars reflecting God's glory and imaging him in wisdom, in rule, and in judgment. Michael watches over God's people until the resurrection. Thus the fate of the one like a son of man, who receives the kingdom, and the fate of the saints of the Most High, who are persecuted, die, and are resurrected, are one and the same. As it is for them, so it is for him; as it is for him, so it is for them.

I tell you the truth, whoever hears my word and believes him who sent me has eternal life and will not be condemned; he has crossed over from death to life. I tell you the truth, a time is coming and has now come when the dead will hear the voice of the Son of God and those who hear will live. For as the Father has life in himself, so he has granted the Son to have life in himself. And he has given him authority to judge because he is the Son of Man.

Do not be amazed at this, for a time is coming when all who are in their graves will hear his voice and come out—those who have done good will rise to live, and those who have done evil will rise to be condemned. (John 5:24–29)

Brothers, we do not want you to be ignorant about those who fall asleep, or to grieve like the rest of men, who have no hope. We believe that Jesus died and rose again and so we believe that God will bring with Jesus those who have fallen asleep in him. According to the Lord's own word, we tell you that we who are still alive, who are left till the coming of the Lord, will certainly not precede those who have fallen asleep. For the Lord himself will come down from heaven, with a loud command, with the voice of the archangel and with the trumpet call of God, and the dead in Christ will rise first. After that, we who are still alive and are left will be caught up together with them in the clouds to meet the Lord in the air. And so we will be with the Lord forever. Therefore encourage each other with these words. (1 Thess. 4:13–18)

Then I saw a great white throne and him who was seated on it. Earth and sky fled from his presence, and there was no place for them. And I saw the dead, great and small, standing before the throne, and books were opened. Another book was opened, which is the book of life. The dead were judged according to what they had done as recorded in the books. The sea gave up the dead that were in it, and death and Hades gave up the dead that were in them, and each person was judged according to what he had done. Then death and Hades were thrown into the lake of fire. The lake of fire is the second death. If anyone's name was not found written in the book of life, he was thrown into the lake of fire.

Then I saw a new heaven and a new earth, for the first heaven and the first earth had passed away, and there was no longer any sea. I saw the Holy City, the new Jerusalem, coming down out of heaven from God, prepared as a bride beautifully dressed for her husband. And I heard a loud voice from the throne saying, "Now the dwelling of God is with men, and he will live with them. They will be his people, and God himself will be with them and be their God. He will wipe every tear from their eyes. There will be no more death or mourning or crying or pain, for the old order of things has passed away."

He who was seated on the throne said, "I am making everything new!" Then he said, "Write this down, for these words are trustworthy and true." (Rev. 20:11–21:5)

FOR FURTHER REFLECTION

1. How does your wisdom shine through in the face of adversity?
2. Do world events inspire doubt in your heart? How do you handle this doubt?
3. If Daniel 11:40–45 describes events before the return of Christ, what will Christians experience (Luke 21:25–28) at that time?

PART FOUR

EPILOGUE

There is one chapter left to study in Daniel. This concludes the breathtaking sweep of history that Daniel puts on display, and ends with a climactic resurrection of the dead and final judgment.

16

HOW LONG UNTIL THE END?

Daniel 12 concludes the book. Daniel echoes the cry of the martyrs throughout history in verse 6, "How long?" After Jesus spoke of the book of Daniel and its fulfillment with respect to the city of Jerusalem, his disciples asked him, "Tell us, when will this happen, and what will be the sign of your coming and of the end of the age?" (Matt. 24:3). When will we see the Son of Man coming in the clouds? How will we know when the hour is nigh? Those who had suffered and died for their testimony also cry out from the altar, "How long before thou wilt judge and avenge our blood on those who dwell upon the earth?" (Rev. 6:10 RSV). Even angels ask the question (Dan. 8:13). The answer, of course, is only what one would expect.

A TIME, TIMES, AND HALF A TIME

The man clothed in linen, who was above the waters of the stream, raised his right hand and his left hand toward heaven; and I heard him swear by him who lives for ever that it would be for a time, two times, and half a time; and that when the shattering of the power of the holy people comes to an end all these things would be accomplished. (12:7 RSV)

The saints must endure for a time, times, and half a time. The second half of the seventieth week of years is the present point in human history. Today, there is nothing of eschatological importance yet to be fulfilled except the coming of Christ to render judgment.

However, Daniel is not satisfied with this answer. He does not "understand"—*bin*, a sapiential word. The one in bright linen, reflecting God's glory, standing above the waters, gives more information to help calculate the times. He sets the calendar at 1,290 days between two events, or about 3? years plus half a month. He then blesses those waiting for the 1,335 days—about another month and a half.

Daniel adds these "zingers" at the end of his book. Just when the reader feels comfortable with Daniel's message, has settled on one of the seven views of chapter 9, and is ready for the book to end, we learn about 1,290 and 1,335 days, and we despair. The critics suggest that the writer expected the end after 1,290 days; but that prediction was premature, so the date was pushed upwards to 1,335.[1] Every so often a group of Christians decides that the end is calculable, and they wait for the Lord on the top of a hill. But Jesus said he would come when unexpected, and he meant it. Did a similar phenomenon happen in the second century B.C.? Is that why the numbers keep revising upwards? No. This implies a second-century date for the composition of Daniel, which all but overlaps its translation into Greek. The book would not have gained canonical status in the Qumran community that soon, especially if the predictions were patently false!

A better explanation is not forthcoming—but this is purposeful. The cryptic numbers leave the reader befuddled. These bolts out of the blue shock Daniel's audience into a state of confusion. The mysterious character of the future is established. Daniel ends with an uninterpreted *raz*. How better to get the point across: "Don't think you understand, because you don't! Just be faithful and persevere, and God will carry you through!"

THE WISE

Throughout history to the end of time, the principles of the paradigmatic first chapter of Daniel apply. Pagans will be in confusion and depend upon the wisdom of their culture, will "run to and fro, and knowledge shall increase" (12:4 RSV). But the wise will shine like stars. "Many shall purify themselves, and make themselves white, and be refined; but the wicked shall do wickedly; and none of the wicked shall understand; but those who are wise shall understand" (12:10 RSV). Almost the last thought in Daniel is the preeminence and significance of wisdom. Throughout it all, the wise will be known, will be comforted, will understand enough to persevere, and will in the end be vindicated and glorified.

When Jesus had finished teaching in parables (Matt. 13:54), the people marveled, "Where did this man get this wisdom?" The parables reveal his wisdom, as do his miracles (Mark 6:2). They are the *raz* of Jesus, and he also provides the *pesher*. Jesus is one greater than Solomon for wisdom (Matt. 12:42). "I will give you words and wisdom that none of your adversaries will be able to resist or contradict" (Luke 21:15). He is the wise man Christians follow and emulate. Christ is Wisdom incarnate for Christians. In him are hidden all the treasures of wisdom and knowledge (Col. 2:3).

It is because of him that you are in Christ Jesus, who has become for us wisdom from God—that is, our righteousness, holiness and redemption. Therefore, as it is written: "Let him who boasts boast in the Lord."

When I came to you, brothers, I did not come with eloquence or superior wisdom as I proclaimed to you the testimony about God. For I resolved to know nothing while I was with you except Jesus Christ and him crucified. (1 Cor. 1:30–2:2)

Since Christ is our wisdom, we should be wise. Paul writes, "Be very careful, then, how you live—not as unwise but as wise, making the most of every opportunity, because the days are evil. Therefore do not be foolish, but understand what the Lord's will is" (Eph. 5:15–17).

In fact, to the world lost in ignorance and sin, Christ is the *Raz* of God—the great mystery (Col. 2:2)—and his death and resurrection are the ultimate apocalyptic events that need explanation, that require a *pesher* to be proclaimed. The great *Pesher* is the gospel—and Christians are tasked with bringing this word of wisdom to the whole world. The folly of the gospel is wiser than the world's wisdom, and God uses it to shame the philosopher of this age (1 Cor. 1:20–27; 2:4; 3:18–20; 4:10). The world bows down to idols of its own making, be they money, pleasure, power, or the wisdom of the Magi. Pagans pray exclusively to Darius for a month. They blaspheme what is sacred to God. They boast in what they make for their own glory. They embark on military campaigns—nation will rise up against nation. They form societies and write new works of "wisdom"—such as the *Humanist Manifesto*. And all along, the wisdom of God is found only with the saints, those who belong to the Son of Man coming with the clouds of heaven.

Be not afraid, O Christian, to speak the words of this wisdom to the world. What can they do to you? If they throw you into the fire, there he is with you. If they cast you with the wild beasts, he is there. If governments wear you out, you have Michael who is stronger than they. You will be vindicated. So shine as stars—for you are the light of the world (Matt. 5:14)—and let them hear the wisdom of God.

FOR FURTHER REFLECTION

1. It is okay not to understand everything. What parts of the Bible are confusing and mysterious to you? But what is the "big picture" of the Bible that you *do* understand clearly?
2. What in the world is mysterious to you?
3. What will you do when an interpreter claims to know the calendar of the end of the world?

CONCLUDING THOUGHTS

Our study of the book of Daniel is now concluded, but it is beneficial to review all that we have encountered. The story begins with a great tragedy, the destruction of Jerusalem and the temple, the dragging of the people of the living God into a foreign land. There Daniel and his friends impressed the despot with their God-given wisdom and were rewarded with high positions of influence in government.

God shook up the tyrant with a terrible dream—which the wisdom of the Magi was unable to explain. Only the faithful Daniel had the answers to what ailed the king. Although oppressed, the saints again found favor; the wisdom of God was displayed, making foolish the wisdom of the world.

The king rejected this revelation from God and demanded that the entire world do so also. God vindicated the saints again in the end, by sending the Son of God to deliver from the flames.

God would not abide this recalcitrant king, and warned him in advance of a terrible judgment. The only one able to advise the king was the believer in the true and living God—again, vindicated in the end.

A blasphemous king followed and was again warned in advance by the saints before the judgment fell.

After this, one last story is told to nail down the salient point that despots and kingdoms seek to supplant God and claim for themselves the divine prerogative. Once more,

Daniel's faithful service to his God is vindicated in the end. The oft-repeated point is obvious—serve the Lord faithfully your life long and you will be vindicated!

This is followed by visions of the future, taking the saints through wars and great suffering until the final Reversal—the Resurrection of the dead, to which the deliverance from the pits of fire and lions pointed.

So every Christian can rest assured that although there will be wars and rumors of wars, terrorists and persecutions, arrogant claims of nations, empty promises, false wisdom, and man claiming divinity, in the end the Christians' faith will be vindicated. So hold firm, endure to the end, and you will be saved.

Amen, and amen. Come, Lord Jesus!

NOTES

CHAPTER ONE: HOW TO READ DANIEL

1. This chiasm is from A. Lenglet, "La Structure Littéraire de Daniel 2–7," *Biblica* 53 (1972): 169–90.
2. There are also two instances of quoted correspondence in Ezra and a single verse in Jeremiah.

CHAPTER TWO: WHY NARRATIVE? WHY APOCALYPTIC?

1. James A. Montgomery, *Daniel*, International Critical Commentary (Edinburgh: T. & T. Clark, 1927), 66–76.
2. Tremper Longman III, *Fictional Akkadian Autobiography* (Winona Lake, Ind.: Eisenbrauns, 1991), 189.
3. John J. Collins, "Inspiration or Illusion: Biblical Theology and the Book of Daniel," *Ex Auditu* 6 (1990): 36.
4. Stephen Miller, *Daniel*, New American Commentary (Nashville: Broadman and Holman, 1994), 318.

CHAPTER THREE: DANIEL AS A WISDOM BOOK

1. John Day, "The Daniel of Ugarit and Ezekiel and the Hero of the Book of Daniel," *Vestus Testamentum* 30 (1980): 182.
2. And its cognate, *patar*.
3. Gerhard von Rad, *Old Testament Theology*, trans. D. M. G. Stalker (New York: Harper & Row, 1965), 2:302.
4. Ibid.
5. John J. Collins, "The Sage in the Apocalyptic and Pseudepigraphic Literature," in *The Sage in Israel and the Ancient Near East*, ed. John G. Gammie (Winona Lake, Ind.: Eisenbrauns, 1990), 347.

CHAPTER FOUR: THE PARADIGM

1. Tremper Longman III, *Daniel*, NIV Application Commentary (Grand Rapids: Zondervan, 1999), 53: "Their robust appearance, usually attained by a rich fare of meats and wine, is miraculously achieved through a diet of vegetables. Only God could have done it." Longman argues that this proves their success is not attributable to the Babylonians.

2. Zdravko Stefanovic, "Daniel: A Book of Significant Reversals," *Andrews University Seminary Studies* 30 (1992): 139–50.

3. Or, "the divine lady."

4. William Shea, "Bel(te)shazzar Meets Belshazzar," *Andrews University Seminary Studies* 26 (1988): 67–81.

5. John Calvin, *Daniel*, Old Testament Commentary 20, trans. by T. H. L. Parker (Grand Rapids: Eerdmans, 1993), 21.

CHAPTER FIVE: NEBUCHADNEZZAR'S HEAD

1. Joyce G. Baldwin, *Daniel*, Tyndale Old Testament Commentaries (Downers Grove, Ill.: InterVarsity, 1975), 123.

2. A. Leo Oppenheim, "The Interpretation of Dreams in the Ancient Near East," *Transactions of the American Philosophical Society*, n.s., 46, (1956): 219.

3. See John H. Walton, "The Four Kingdoms of Daniel, *Journal of the Evangelical Theological Society* 29 (1986): 25–36. Walton presents an evangelical argument for the four kingdoms of Assyria, Media, Medo-Persia, and Greece.

4. Tremper Longman III, *Daniel*, (Grand Rapids: Zondervan, 1999), 82.

5. John Goldingay, *Daniel*, Word Biblical Commentary 30 (Waco, Tex.: Word, 1989), 58.

CHAPTER SIX: NEBUCHADNEZZAR'S FEAT

1. Hector I. Avalos, "The Comedic Function of the Enumerations of Officials and Instruments in Daniel 3," *Catholic Biblical Quarterly* 53 (1991): 581.

CHAPTER SEVEN: NEBUCHADNEZZAR'S STUMP (INSANITY)

1. R. K. Harrison, *Introduction to the Old Testament* (Grand Rapids: Eerdmans, 1969), 1116. Despite Harrison's firsthand account,

"monomania," "boanthropy," and "lycanthropy" are not clinical diagnostic categories in *The Diagnostic and Statistical Manual of Mental Disorders: DSM-IV-R*, 4th ed. (Washington, D.C.: American Psychiatric Association, 1987).

2. Joyce G. Baldwin, *Daniel* (Downers Grove, Ill.: InterVarsity, 1975), 110.

3. Sinclair B. Ferguson, *Daniel* (Waco, Tex.: Word, 1988), 102.

4. Baldwin, *Daniel*, 116.

5. It is probably a mistake to interpret the imagery here on the basis of the parable of the sower, which might suggest that the birds represent Satan and the tree might be the bloated institutional church harboring reprobates and heretics. That reading ignores the imagery in Daniel.

CHAPTER EIGHT: THE HANDWRITING ON THE WALL

1. A. Lenglet, "La Structure Littéraire de Daniel 2–7," *Biblica* 53 (1972): 169–90.

2. John Calvin, *Daniel*, trans. T. H. L. Parker, Old Testament Commentary 20 (Grand Rapids: Eerdmans, 1993), 208–9.

3. See Joyce G. Baldwin, *Daniel* (Downers Grove, Ill.: InterVarsity, 1975), 123. Baldwin argues that the event does have such an explanation: the king's fear of Cyrus, and a drunken fantasy of human fingers pathologically transformed an ordinary steward's note into an object of terror.

4. The following analysis is taken substantially from David Brewer, "*Mene, Mene, Teqel, Uparsin*: Daniel 5:25 in Cuneiform," *Tyndale Bulletin* 42 (1991): 310–16.

5. The following material is taken from Kim Monroe, *Daniel 5*, cassette WBS 6/26, New Life Cassettes, 2003.

6. Baldwin, *Daniel*, 120.

7. The following is taken substantially from Al Wolters, "Untying the King's Knots: Physiology and Wordplay in Daniel 5," *Journal of Biblical Literature* 110 (1991): 117–22.

8. Ibid., 121.

CHAPTER NINE: WORSHIPPING MAN

1. Herbert Schlossberg, *Idols for Destruction* (Nashville: Nelson, 1983), 47.

2. Francis Schaeffer and C. Everett Koop, *Whatever Happened to the Human Race?* (Wheaton, Ill.: Crossway, 1983).

3. Dana Nolan Fewell, *Circle of Sovereignty* (Nashville: Abingdon, 1991), 10.

CHAPTER TEN: THE CLOUD RIDER

1. Tremper Longman III, *Daniel* (Grand Rapids: Zondervan, 1999), 190.

2. For further development of this theme, see Tremper Longman III and Daniel Reid, *God Is a Warrior* (Grand Rapids: Zondervan, 1995).

3. Much in this discussion is taken from Vern Poythress, "The Holy Ones of the Most High in Daniel VII," *Vetus Testamentum* 26 (1976): 208–13.

4. Jane Schaberg, "Daniel 7, 12 and the New Testament Passion-Resurrection Predictions," *New Testament Studies* 31 (1985): 208–22.

CHAPTER ELEVEN: THE PENULTIMATE LITTLE HORN

1. Daniel 7:8 reads *qeren 'ahari ze'erah*, "another small horn," while 8:9 reads *qeren 'ahat mitse'irah*, "another horn from littleness," seemingly a purposeful distinction. It would have been a simple matter to word these alike if the reader were meant to equate the two. Some scholars emend the text to forge just such an equation.

2. Richard Patterson, "The Key Role of Daniel 7," *Grace Theological Journal* 12 (1991): 245–61.

3. Interestingly, commentators who explain Nebuchadnezzar's dreams on psychological grounds do not diagnose Daniel here, although he exhibits symptoms of mental illness!

CHAPTER THIRTEEN: THE HANDWRITING ON THE SCROLL

1. Harold W. Hoehner, *Bibliotheca Sacra* 132 (1975): 47–65.

2. James A. Montgomery, *Daniel*, International Critical Commentary (Edinburgh: T. & T. Clark, 1927), 397.

3. C. F. Keil, *The Book of the Prophet Daniel* (Edinburgh: T. & T. Clark, 1877), 389.

4. Meredith Kline, "The Covenant of the Seventieth Week." In *The Law and the Prophets*, ed. John Skilton (Nutley, N.J.: Presbyterian and Reformed, 1974), 452–69.

5. E. J. Young, *The Messianic Prophecies of Daniel* (Grand Rapids: Eerdmans, 1954), 66–78.

6. Sinclair B. Ferguson, *Daniel* (Waco: Word, 1988), 203.

7. Tremper Longman III, *Daniel* (Grand Rapids: Zondervan, 1999), 225–30.

CHAPTER FIFTEEN: WAR ON EARTH

1. See also Joyce G. Baldwin, *Daniel* (Downers Grove, Ill.: InterVarsity, 1975); and Tremper Longman III, *Daniel* (Grand Rapids: Zondervan, 1999).

2. C. F. Keil, *The Book of the Prophet Daniel* (Edinburgh: T. & T. Clark, 1877), 466.

CHAPTER SIXTEEN: HOW LONG UNTIL THE END?

1. John J. Collins, "Inspiration or Illusion: Biblical Theology and the Book of Daniel," *Ex Auditu* 6 (1990): 34: "The most plausible explanation . . . is that the date was recalculated when the first number expired."

FOR FURTHER READING

Adams, Jay E. *The Time Is at Hand*. Philadelphia: Presbyterian and Reformed, 1966.

Avalos, Hector I. "The Comedic Function of the Enumerations of Officials and Instruments in Daniel 3." *Catholic Biblical Quarterly* 53 (1991): 580–88.

Baldwin, Joyce G. *Daniel*. Tyndale Old Testament Commentaries. Downers Grove, Ill.: InterVarsity, 1975.

Brewer, David. *"Mene, Mene, Teqel, Uparsin*: Daniel 5:25 in Cuneiform." *Tyndale Bulletin* 42 (1991): 310–16.

Calvin, John. *Daniel*. Old Testament Commentary 20. Translated by T. H. L. Parker. Grand Rapids: Eerdmans, 1993.

Camping, Harold. *1994*. New York: Vantage, 1992.

Day, John. "The Daniel of Ugarit and Ezekiel and the Hero of the Book of Daniel." *Vetus Testamentum* 30 (1980): 174–84.

The Diagnostic and Statistical Manual of Mental Disorders: DSM-III-R. 4th ed. Washington, D.C.: American Psychiatric Association, 1987.

Driver, S. R. *Daniel*. Cambridge: Cambridge University Press, 1936.

Ferguson, Sinclair B. *Daniel*. Waco, Tex.: Word, 1988.

Fewell, Danna Nolan. *Circle of Sovereignty*. Nashville: Abingdon, 1991.

Goldingay, John. *Daniel*. Word Biblical Commentary 30. Dallas: Word Books, 1989.

———. " 'Holy Ones on High' in Daniel 7:18." *Journal for the Study of the Old Testament* 107 (1988): 495–501.

Harrison, R. K. *Introduction to the Old Testament*. Grand Rapids: Eerdmans, 1969.

Keil, C. F. *The Book of the Prophet Daniel*. Biblical Commentary on the Old Testament. Translated by M. G. Easton. Edinburgh: T. & T. Clark, 1877.

Lenglet, A. "La Structure Littéraire de Daniel 2–7." *Biblica* 53 (1972): 169–90.

Longman, Tremper, III. *Daniel*. NIV Application Commentary. Grand Rapids: Zondervan, 1999.

———. *Fictional Akkadian Autobiography*. Winona Lake, Ind.: Eisenbrauns, 1991.

———, and Daniel Reid. *God Is a Warrior*. Grand Rapids: Zondervan, 1995.

Miller, Stephen. *Daniel*. New American Commentary. Nashville: Broadman and Holman, 1994.

Montgomery, James A. *Daniel*. International Critical Commentary. Edinburgh: T. & T. Clark, 1927.

Newsom, Carol A. "The Past as Revelation: History in Apocalyptic Literature." *Quarterly Review* 4 (1984): 40–53.

Oppenheim, A. Leo. "The Interpretation of Dreams in the Ancient Near East." *Transactions of the American Philosophical Society*, n.s., 46 (1956): 179–373.

Patterson, Richard. "The Key Role of Daniel 7." *Grace Theological Journal* 12 (1991): 245–61.

Poythress, Vern S. "The Holy Ones of the Most High in Daniel VII." *Vetus Testamentum* 26 (1976): 208–13.

Pritchard, James B. *Ancient Near Eastern Texts Relating to the Old Testament*. Princeton: Princeton University Press, 1950.

Raabe, Paul R. "Daniel 7: Its Structure and Role in the Book." *Hebrew Annual Review* 9 (1985): 267–75.

Rowley, H. H. "Meaning of Daniel for Today." *Interpretation* 15 (1961): 387–97.

Schaberg, Jane. "Daniel 7, 12 and the New Testament Passion-Resurrection Predictions." *New Testament Studies* 31 (1985): 208–22.

Schaeffer, Francis, and C. Everett Koop. *Whatever Happened to the Human Race?* Wheaton, Ill.: Crossway, 1983.

Schlossberg, Herbert. *Idols for Destruction.* Nashville: Nelson, 1983.

Shea, William. "Bel(te)shazzar Meets Belshazzar." *Andrews University Seminary Studies* 26 ('1988): 67–81.

Stefanovic, Zdravko. "Daniel: A Book of Significant Reversals." *Andrews University Seminary Studies* 30 (1992): 139–50.

Wolters, Al. "Untying the King's Knots: Physiology and Wordplay in Daniel 5." *Journal of Biblical Literature* 110 (1991): 117–22.

Young, E. J. *The Prophecy of Daniel.* Grand Rapids: Eerdmans, 1949.

INDEX OF SCRIPTURE